MW00896071

West Hillsborough Origins
Stories & Poems by a Native Son

Charles B. Stanley

Mike, it was great
meeting a new author.
Enjoy.
Charles B. Stanley
5/19/18

Published by: The Create Short Book Writers Project
Wayne H. Drumheller, Editor and Founder
Distribution in the USA by and www. amazon.com

ISBN-13:978-1986483308
ISBN-10-1986483304

Contents

This book is dedicated to the Hillsboro High School Class of 1958.

Introduction

Standing on the precipice of Occoneechee Mountain in central North Carolina, one can see the western most part of the town of Hillsborough: a river meandering below, a railroad track and perhaps hear the sound of a distant freight. To me, I see the origins of my seven decades of time-space on this planet. Travel with me as I share poems and stories of West Hillsborough and beyond.

From where I am standing, we can clamber down the south side of the Occoneechee cliff. There is an almost-hidden path as we scramble holding onto underbrush. We will faintly smell fern and musky mushrooms as we get closer to the hidden destination.

THE PANTHER'S DEN

In a favorite spot of my childhood
Musky mushrooms and fern abound
There, a tiny cave is nestled under the wood
Where a trickling spring is the only sound.

In legend the cave housed a wary cat
That crouched above the rocky mound;
Then moved above where a resting man sat
Where a trickling spring was the only sound.

The surprised man with terror in his face
Arose to meet the fury's leap.
The gun shattered the quiet of that place
As the fierce feline fell in a lifeless heap.

The Eno meanders far below;
Animal trails that children found
Lead us back to long ago
Where a trickling spring is the only sound.

My wife's grandmother Mae Jackson Thompson, right, and friend Bessie Terrell on a Sunday afternoon hike to the Panther's Den in the early 1900's. People have enjoyed hiking to the Panther's Den for generations.

Generations have enjoyed visiting the Panther's Den.
Pictured are Laura Stanley and Tonya Overman

Leaving the Panther's Den and following the path beneath the cliff and above the Eno River, you get a sense of place; the river almost speaks as it moves slowly along.

THE RIVER SPEAKS

The river runs there.
Meandering through the vale;
Birds flitter through the air.
And I listen to its tale.

It speaks in voice so low
As it glides along the way,
Murmuring of long, long ago
Of a distant ancient day.

"Long before any men came
I gave life to others:
The fox, bear, and other game.
Then they were free brothers.

Then I saw his face
Upon my shimmering breast.
Reddish was his race--
The forerunner of the rest."

The Eno River as seen from the Riverwalk in Hillsborough.

ENO

Eno, the Indian saw in you his face
As he hunted for deer and bear.
Now he is gone from this wooded place;
Somehow, it doesn't seem fair.

"His name is upon the waters; ye may not wash it out,"
Was said to us of old.
About the first ones, the strong, the stout.
Eno, if you could speak, what stories would be told.

O River, what secrets you hold!
What happened to those who gave you name?
Your answers are worth more than gold,
But silently you stay forever the same.

REFLECTIONS FROM THE RAILROAD

In West Hillsborough, looking north at the West Hill Avenue intersection with the railroad, one would today see a house on the left. In my mind's eye, I envision it as it was more than 50 years ago---the old C.E. Riley grocery store but better known to me as Betty Riley's store. Betty was an attractive woman, the daughter of C.E. Riley who had died several years earlier leaving her the store. Later, she would marry Fred Seagroves. It was a bustling place where you could get groceries and about anything else needed. Mom never hesitated to send me there when she ran out of flour or tea. The store was a checker player's heaven. During the winter, grizzled old fellows played right inside the store with the large glass windows giving them a projection encompassing their outside world. In summer months the competition moved to the back porch of the store. Surrounded by empty boxes and the warm summer breeze, these guys spent hours and hours calculating the moves of friendly adversaries. I remember one sweltering summer day lingering on that porch. I watched what to me was not exactly invigorating action taking place between Dad and Mr. John Midgett, the insurance salesman. There was an old pole holding up one corner of the porch roof.

I was leaning against it when I became aware that my index finger had somehow gotten stuck in an insignificant drilled hole. Perhaps if I had been older than nine at the time, a plan of escape would have come to fruition; however, I just stood there with my thoughts of doom--What if I never get my finger loose? Maybe someone will have to come and saw off the pole to free me and what if the entire roof then comes down on my head? I tugged and twisted, and then I tugged and twisted some more. The cardboard cut-out of Lola Albright drinking Coca Cola perched on the back porch stared smilingly down on my futile efforts. The 3:00 whistle at the Cone Mill Eno Plant pierced the air and reverberated and echoed all around me. Soon Dad would say that it was time to go home and help Mom fix supper. She would be waking from working the third shift from 11:00pm-7:00am.

My predicament was compounded when several of those first shift workers emerged from within the store, Pepsis in hand, to watch the checker competition. None noticed me standing there leaning against the pole. If they had only known my agony within and without. I don't remember how or exactly when, but somehow about that time my finger slipped free. Dad never knew about my misery or the excitement of my escape. Just remember, no matter how bleak the future looks, there is always a better day ahead. Also, always be careful about sticking your fingers in the wrong places. I was lucky. I got mine back.

The building on the right was the Riley meat market. In the distance you see the building that was Betty Riley's store, 2018.

Balancing on the rail of the track and covering about 200 yards walking east toward the depot, one can see the old church on the left. Facing the tracks and the once thriving mill village on the other side, Eno United Methodist Church majestically stands as a sentinel to the past.

Time changes the geographical landscape. During the 1950's Cone Mill was faced with putting indoor plumbing in the houses of the Eno mill village. Rather than tackle that problem, Cone gave employees the opportunity to buy the homes for twenty-five dollars a room, provided they would pay to have the houses moved to another location. It became an everyday occurrence to see a house moving down the road.

Now, more than 60 years later, nature has reclaimed what was once its own. One can go to the old village site today and find sidewalks hidden beneath the foliage. Going from one level to another, cement steps, reminiscent of Inca ruins, lead present explorers to nowhere. The present Sunday School building adjacent to Eno church was one of those houses. It is almost like the church took one of its children and pulled it up close as a reminder of a childhood long ago. Doug Marlette, in his novel, The Bridge, remarks: "The mill village is still there. It's just hidden under the kudzu." The village is still there for me and it is hidden under the "kudzu" of my mind.

Looking west toward Dimmocks Mills Road. Note the clothes on the line and the outhouses. In 1953 Eno Cotton Mill provided 148 houses without indoor plumbing for its workers.

My wife's uncle Errol Thompson. You can see Eno Church facing the Mill Village

A landscape changed by time. Our cover photo taken in the late 1940's or mid 1950's of snowfall on the mill village.

The mill houses were moved in 1956. In 2018 the railroad tracks now have warning signals but no mill village houses exist on that side of Dimmock's Mill Road.

DID YOU EVER WALK A RAIL

Did you ever walk a rail
From the depot to the mill;
And make popsicle sticks sail,
Or follow a bark boat until
          it ran into the river?

Did you ever chase bats with a cane pole;
Or bomb an enemy from the apple tree?
How about chasing a squirrel from a hole?
Could you make a rock skip one, two, three
          across the river?

Did you make the Sunday outing a treat
And climb to the top of the ridge?
En route trod with bare feet
Across the dusty, hot bridge
          that spanned the river?

Did you ever roll on the church yard grass
And look up at clouds and birds on wing
And feel time's pendulum pass
Like naked youth on the swing
          out over the river?

Walking the rail is a family tradition.

HILLSBOROUGH--WEST

Ninety-foot trestle, Coon Rock
And the Depot;
Memory words from Hillsborough-West

The Dam; New Hill; Sandy Beach--The Eno's flow;
Old Hill; the Cliff; Home--that stands out best.

Monkey Bottom; West End; and
Betty Riley's store;
Bellevue; Seven Mile Creek,
And Eno Mill.
A haircut from a booster seat
Far above the floor
In Ross Taylor's barbership
Next to Bozo's Grill.

Church of God; Eno Methodist;
And West Hill Baptist, too
Welcomed Sunday's clean and fine
The 11:20 train that always came through
And destroyed sermons time after time.

The Barracks; the Rock Quarry; Old Dimmocks Mill;
The First Bridge; the Second
Bridge; and the Panther's Den;
The Mountain; Two Room Row;
And Daughtery's Hill--

It's great to go back with
Thoughts, paper, and pen.

The Stanley Home Place

The smokehouse located behind the home place.

EARLY WEST HILLSBOROUGH MEMORIES

Perhaps here I should give the reader a description of my family make-up. Mom and Dad had both been married previously. Mom was married to Lillard Medlin and Dad was married to Sally Lindley. Both spouses died. Dad's name was Charles Bell Stanley, the same as mine. Mom's name was Myrtle. Her maiden name was Ray. Mom had four children: Frances, Phyllis, Thomas, and Mary Lou. Dad had two children: Buford and Pansy. Buford attended the Naval Academy in Annapolis. Pansy died of a cerebral hemorrhage the day I was brought home from the hospital. I remember people telling me how torn he was; being so distraught at the death of his daughter, and on the other hand being happy with the birth of a son. That must have been some ordeal. Dad was 57 when I was born and my mom was in her late 30's.

The very first thing I remember was a terrible accident involving my sister, Mary Lou. When she was thirteen, our brother-in-law Lawrence "Peck" Albright, was making a potato storage bin in the old smokehouse when a nail he was driving flew up and pierced her eye. I can still picture Momma pulling the dress over her head to take her to the hospital. I was three at the time.

Other early memories are associated with World War II. I remember my brother, Thomas, coming up to the back porch. He was wearing his uniform and I remember jumping into his arms. It's funny that I don't ever remember any such embrace with him at any other time in my life. Somewhere in that same time frame, I remember the family gathering around an old Victrola and listening to a recorded message from Thomas that he had sent home from wherever he had been stationed. I wonder what ever happened to that recording and was it a common occurrence? I do remember Momma was crying when she heard his voice.

World War II brought with it, for me, a fear of airplanes. I can remember trying to get into the house when I heard one approaching. It has always seemed like a cruel trick for Thomas to have locked the doors when I tried to escape to my home. Later I just dug up the yard creating foxholes in which to hide. There are probably indentions today in the yard of the old homeplace.

The railroad came within 200 yards of my house and the "sound of the outward bound" made a lasting impression. Troop trains with sister Mary Lou chasing alongside and the soldiers yelling at her comes to mind. Train car after train car carrying tanks, jeeps, and other military supplies came by everyday while I watched from the front steps of Eno Methodist Church that faced not only the railroad but the mill village on the other side of the tracks.

I remember my fifth birthday. All the church bells were ringing in the neighborhood and car horns were blowing. I was so pleased that everyone was glad that it was my birthday. Later I realized that May 8, 1945 was the day the Germans surrendered, ending that phase of World War II.

I wonder if most people remember their first bicycle. My memory is one of a Christmas snow and sitting on the seat of the bicycle on my back porch being very unhappy because I could not ride it. Any other time I would have been excited over a white Christmas, but not that one.

In my mind's eye, probably when I was about five, I see several men on a summer evening standing outside our bedroom window. Our radio was adjacent to the open screened window and I remember hearing someone say, "Joe Louis is fighting tonight." Could it be in the mid 1940's there were people who didn't have radios that would have to come to a neighbor's house to hear the fight through an open window? Perhaps they were just having a "boxing match" get together. Probably it was like tailgating without the food. Maybe there was a drink or two.

This reminds me of my childhood radio shows. I guess the most impressive to me was "The Lone Ranger." With his faithful Indian friend, Tonto; a cloud of dust and a hearty "High Ho Silver," I travel back to those thrilling days of yesteryear. I had a bike that I named Silver even though it was red. Who could ever forget the sound of the creaking door in "The Inner Sanctum." Terror came into my room at night in the time before child ratings. Of course there was "Fibber McGee and Mollie." I still remember they lived on Wistful Vista Drive. Mom always listened to "Ma Perkins" and "Portia Faces Life." Every evening we tuned in to "One Man's Family" and heard the announcer say, "Tonight we are listening to Book 23, chapter 9 in the life of One Man's Family." The sound of the whine of an angry stinging insect precluded the beginning of "The Green Hornet" with his valet, Kato. The news was always brought to you by H.V. Kathenborne. He was the Walter Cronkite of his day. Nothing could beat the imagination that radio brought to our lives. I remember an episode of "The Lone Ranger" when he came to town disguised as an old man. The sound of his aged feet shuffling on the wooden streets of the town was very convincing. When he gathered the information he needed, the resounding sound of the strong footsteps of our hero of yesterday echoed iconically through my mind, and I can still recall the sound today. I was somewhat disappointed when Clayton Moore played the Lone Ranger role on television. On the radio he was immortal. TV just didn't provide the imaginative thrill given to us by the radio.

Dad was a boxing fan. We were not the first in the neighborhood to get a television. To my best recollection, "Wednesday Night Fights" were sponsored by Pabst Blue Ribbon and the Friday night contests were brought commercial wise by Gillette razor blades. On Wednesday night we went to George Dabb's house which was about one block east of Allen Ruffin Avenue. The house may have been owned by the Spoons. Mable was George's sister-in-law. Her brother, Junior, was usually there smoking a big cigar. George worked at the train depot. I remember jokingly asking him, "George, when does the 7:00 train run?" He would reply: "Charles, sometime around 7:30 if we're lucky." Those were fun times. I guess I was about ten years old and felt a bond with those guys. I collected Ring Magazine issues and would cut out pictures of my favorite boxers and put them on the wall. I could name the top ten fighters in about every weight division. I knew about their families and their records.

Mom always said that Dad missed a lot, meaning there were some things he was really oblivious about. On Friday nights Dad would take me to Jim Faucette's house to watch the Friday Night Fights. I remember one evening being aware of people going to bed while Dad and I sat there. He never seemed to get the hint that it was time to go home. Maybe Mom was right. Lynda, to this day thinks I picked up some traits of my dad. Oh, well, perhaps ignorance really is bliss. Later, when we got our first television set, the test pattern took up part of the day. Dad always tried to adjust the television by smacking it on the top or jiggling a few knobs, with the hope that his efforts would make the test pattern go away. I remember WFMY Channel 2 as being the first area station. When 11:00pm came, the national anthem was played and then the test pattern appeared and remained until programming returned at 6:00am. My, how times have changed.

My father, Charles B. Stanley, Sr.

THE RIVER RAN THROUGH US

Many of us West Hillsboro kids learned to swim in the Eno River. There were other places like Sparrow's Pool in Chapel Hill, Hogan's Lake, or the annual church summer trip to Pullen Park in Raleigh, but each of those excursions were away from the neighborhood.

The river ran through us. There was a mountain swimming hole located at the base of the towering quarry cliff. I can picture a rope swing there. That's where most of the mountain village guys swam.

Up the river a ways on the other side between the Eno Mill Bridge and the Coon Rock was Sandy Beach. That's where I learned to swim. Why they called it Sandy Beach I'll never know. All I remember was a make-shift ladder, the proverbial rope swing, and of course, the feeling of mud squishing between your toes on the bottom of the river – no sand.

Clothing was always optional and often no option at all. Most of the New Hill and the Old Hill guys swam there. There were stories of older brothers taking younger siblings, throwing them in the water, and yelling, "Okay you gotta sink or swim!" I don't remember anyone drowning there and that method for teaching youngsters to swim is very motivational.

I never saw anyone swimming at the Coon Rock, but there is a story about Freck Dollar diving off the top of the rock into the shallow water and actually breaking some bones in his neck. He walked around quite a while with one of those neck braces. One would hear, "Did you know that Freck broke his neck at the Coon Rock?"

Before the Ben Johnson Dam was built at the First Bridge, the old Dimmocks Mill rock dam stood for many years. I remember as a young kid some people swimming there. I believe it was Evelyn Cox who screamed as she floated by me in the shallow water, "I found a tick! I found a tick!" I must have been about 6 years old at the time. Funny how you don't forget some things.

Dad liked to fish at the Coon Rock. He was a patient fisherman and could sit there all day. He would put dough on his hook with that old cane pole and fish for what he called suckers. He said he never wanted to go to the ocean and fish because he was told that you just had to throw in your line and a fish would bite the bait right away. He thought that would have taken all of the fun out of it, so he sat, and he sat, and he sat. I don't think it would bother him if he sat all day and got nothing. He said it was all in the anticipation of what might happen.

I am not much of a fisherman but I did have some fun times. One exciting experience happened under the Second Bridge. That is the one up past the Ben Johnson Dam. If you are standing on the Second Bridge and look north, you can see the 90-foot trestle where the cow made a famous plunge but that story is to come.

Back to the fishing story. Herley Dickey was the father of Joe and Marvin and he probably wasn't aware that he was a second father to me. I was really overjoyed to be invited on a night fishing venture at the Second Bridge spot. When I got there, Herley brought out several Clorox jugs. We all got busy tying hooks around the top of them and baiting them with huge squirming worms. We three guys got in the rowboat and set the jugs from the bridge all the way down to where the Seven Mile Creek joined up with the Eno. When we got back, Herley had built a fire and we roasted hot dogs and marshmallows. To me, that was a great feast. After about an hour or two, the only light was the full moon that was reflecting off the unforgettable scene of Clorox jugs darting this way and that way up and down the river. Herley said, "OK boys, go get your fish."

We had no idea what we had snared. Joe pulled out a flashlight as we rowed toward the first jug. Grabbing it by the handle, Marvin pulled it out of the water. We all screamed at the time thinking it was a snake, but actually it was an eel. At that moment, I didn't rightly know what the difference was. Later, a huge turtle made it to the bottom of the boat. We were scurrying around trying to get out of its way, almost tipping the boat. Believe it or not, we did catch a mess of fish: brim, small-mouth bass, and catfish. When we got back with our haul, Herley had the frying pan hot and after cleaning the fish, we had quite a meal. We didn't eat the turtle – we turned it and the eel loose.

The 90-foot trestle as seen from the Second Bridge

THE FIRE-CRACKER FIGHT

From the Railroad facing the old church, one can visualize a little shed where years ago, several boys had a club house. Of course there were no girls allowed. In fact there was a sign that read: "No Grils Allowed." Later some little interloping scamp had scribbled beneath, "What about us Grils?" Being the oldest of our motley crew, I felt I should be president, so I nominated Gene Albright and he was elected unanimously. That wasn't the way it was supposed to be, but that's the way it goes in a democracy. We were somewhat envious regarding the Old Hill Gang on the other side of the tracks, because they had been seen building a log cabin down beside the Eno River. We decided as a group to go over and dismantle the cabin. I don't remember who initiated the plan, but it was probably Jackie Feltman, the preacher's kid. He was always getting us into trouble and somehow coming out smelling like a rose. He once shot me in the rear with an air rifle and somehow convinced his mom and dad that he was holding part of the gun and his brother Don was pulling the trigger. Neither was punished. I think his parents thought it was funny. Getting back to the story…

The grass still glistened from the July morning shower as the four of us crawled into the tarp covered "clubhouse." The faded "Grils Not Allowed" sign hung precariously over the tiny opening. Today was to be devoted to carrying out the long-time secret plan of destroying the log cabin being built by the Old Hill Gang.

"When do we go, Charles?" Gene asked, looking at his uncle, three years older.

"If Benny and Jackie can get away, we ought to leave here at the sound of the 3:00 Eno Mill whistle."

Our quartet crossed the yard of the Methodist Church just as the whistle sound reverberated from the mill, up the tracks, and into our memories. We ran barefooted across the hot blacktop where the railroad and street intersected. Going directly over the track, we entered the mill village. The tall oak trees kept the dirt streets cool to our feet. Moving quickly, our small band came to the second row of houses and beyond to the two-room row, the final group of homes overlooking the Eno River.

"There's the cabin!" Benny exclaimed.

"Do you see anybody?" Jackie, the preacher's son asked.

No one could be seen near the rough but neatly built structure standing out clearly in the center of a small grassy area about fifty feet from the river. Four boys quietly made their way to the hewn objective. The only sounds were their heartbeats and the quiet murmur of the river.

Nine year old Gene was the first to grab a sapling log and give it a tug. He was quickly joined by the others as they pried and pulled, and slowly the connecting corners began to loosen.

"This end is loose!" yelled, Gene's brother, Benny, and he and I lifted the timber from its mooring and headed for the river. Within fifteen minutes, half of the remaining structure was leaning wobbly while the other half was floating lazily toward who knows where.

"I wonder how long it will take this cabin to float to Durham" mused Gene.

Speculation was quickly changed to confusion and bedlam as the Old Hill Gang suddenly burst into the clearing! Bodies were tumbling all over each other. Shouts of "Don't let them get away," and "Let's beat their butts and throw THEM in the river" echoed off the Occoneechee Mountain and wafted over the village.

I was hurrying up the briar bordered path when suddenly Joe Boy Carroll shouted from behind. Turning I saw my young adversary with a lighted firecracker leaving his hand headed straight for its target. In my memory, everything happened in slow motion: the firecracker tumbling over and over, the stillness of the air, a bird singing somewhere nearby, and the terror of impending doom coming to an explosive climax. More than 60 years have passed since the July fireworks on the river bank, but I can still feel the impact of the ear-ringing blast as the object detonated after slipping down inside my new Sears and Roebuck shirt.

Time erases the particulars of what happened next, but I do recall an ensuing Saturday night when I was taking my weekly bath in the big tin tub next to the kitchen woodstove. Each time Mom or Dad came into the room, I turned my back not only from pre-adolescence embarrassment but mainly to hide the large burn on my chest.

I never told my parents about the episode because of the shame for being in the wrong place doing something that would have disappointed them. Years later, I asked if Joe Boy Carroll remembered that day. He said that he did not remember but apologized anyway.

ELEMENTARY SCHOOL HOLDS MANY MEMORIES

In West Hillsborough, the only remaining vestiges of West Hillsboro Elementary School are two sections. I think one would have been the cafeteria, added some time after I left, and the other possibly an early classroom. Years after I left there the school was closed and turned into an apartment building. Later, the apartments caught fire and burned. All that remains is the rock wall that surrounded the school. The school is gone but a deluge of early memories remain.

My first school memory is being on the back of Thurman Parrish as I attempted to dismount another first grader from the lofty back of another guy. Looking back now, I realize that our mounts were only in the fifth grade and the fall would not have been a great one.

I also remember the view. West Hillsboro Elementary was located on top of a hill and in my young eyes, one could see forever. Maybe this was the first time we began to see that our world was a bigger place than our own back yards. Since there was no cafeteria during the years I attended, we went to the kitchen and carried our food trays back to our classroom. There was a large auditorium used not only by the school, but also churches and other organizations. I remember a talent show, a boxing match, and of course the school holiday programs.

Every Christmas students were shown the Shirley Temple classic, "Heidi." I think I cried every year when her grandfather discovered that she was gone and went searching for her. The last year I was there the film broke – it was probably about time.

The teachers were very instrumental in laying the groundwork for our later lives. I remember Ms Mattie Blackwood (first grade), Mrs. Umstead (second grade). By the way, if one had not completely accomplished his or her first grade work, the student was promoted to High First. Looking back, I don't think those children felt bad about going to the High First. In fact, I was a little envious. For some reason, High First sounded better than second. Getting back to the teachers, Mrs. Cole was the third-grade teacher but I think the year I was in third, she was having a baby and Mrs. Gary Lloyd taught us. I remember a spelling bee we had in the classroom and Bobby Baily won a silver dollar. That would have been a very big deal about 70 years ago. Our fourth grade teacher was Mrs. Remus Smith who was very stern but good. My fifth-grade teacher was Mrs. Gladys Harris. She was also principal of the school. At the end of the fifth grade we were transferred to Hillsboro which had grades 1 through 12. We found ourselves in a combination sixth and seventh grade classroom. Would you believe that after two weeks, a sixth grade was established at West Hillsboro and we went back for our sixth-grade year? Mrs. Harris was our teacher once more.

I entered West Hillsboro Elementary School in 1946. There were no counselors, social workers, or child psychologists. At least they didn't have those titles. We had teachers and I guess they were all of those roles combined. I still have a vivid memory of standing behind a classroom door telling Mrs. Umstead about some serious family problem. The greatest compliment I could give her was she listened. To my knowledge, they all did, and we are eternally grateful because they cared for us.

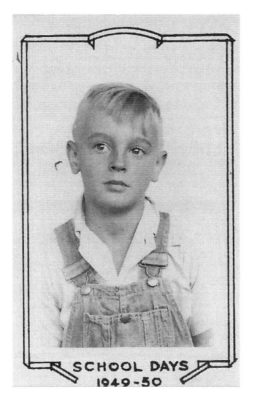

My school picture, 4ᵗʰ grade

The remains of West Hillsboro Elementary

WEST HILLSBOROUGH HAD ITS OWN FIELD OF DREAMS

28995 Lansing Road in Dyersville, Iowa, is an address that most of us do not recognize unless you saw the movie "Field of Dreams" starring Kevin Costner and James Earl Jones. I can still see Shoeless Joe Jackson and others coming out of the cornfield with a background voice, "Build it and they will come." To me, West Hillsborough had its field of dreams; actually there were several. The first wasn't really much of a field; it was a make-shift playing area in front of West Hillsboro Elementary School. There was a huge oak tree at home plate and another at first base. I don't remember what we used for second and third base.

It was probably third grade, 1948, when Wallace King hit a ball all the way up in the maple tree in deep center field. He was so strong and was a benchmark for the rest of us. Over and over one would hear, "Don't you wish you could hit a ball like Wallace King?"

I wonder how many people reading this played baseball on the red-dirt field just on the right past Brooks' store between there and the old water works. Today, the store is gone and the field is hidden in a growth of pine trees. In my field of dreams I see players coming out of those pine trees. I see W.F. Riddle, T.B.Combs, Poley Medlin, Benny Ray Albright, Jasper "Jap" Medlin, Buster Davis, Pud Cole, Joe and Marvin Dickey, David and Wayne Medlin, Pete Oakley, and a host of others. Jap Medlin was one of the most graceful players I have ever seen. You could hit a long fly ball and he would put his glove behind his back and catch it. Try that. For me it was impossible, sometimes even hitting me on the head.

Bryant "Buster" Davis invented a game – at least I think he did. I don't remember anyone else playing it. He would take an old tobacco stick as a bat and give you a stack of bottle caps. You could pitch them to him and we would knock the fire out of them. He set up distances for singles, doubles, triples, and homeruns. When it was your turn to bat, he could make those bottle caps curve so you could never hit them. I can still picture him sitting on the porch at Brooks' store.

Probably the most played-upon field was the one down behind the depot. That's where the mill teams played. I can remember an old-timer's game there and for the first time watching my dad play baseball there. Was there something about the outfield where it sort of dropped off and you couldn't see the batter very well? I have a vague memory of that.

We kids actually played on the little strip of land between Eno Church and the railroad. If you hit a foul ball to the left, it went down the embankment to the tracks. If you hit a foul ball to the right, you possibly could hit a passing motorist. I don't think they would have been in much danger because most of our balls had long lost their covers and were covered in duct tape or maybe nothing at all. We just watched them get smaller and smaller as they slowly unwound. Now if you really hit a ball far down the left field line, it could land in a coal car as the train rumbled past and then travel for about 200 miles.

ALLEN RUFFIN AVENUE REMEMBERED

While standing on the railroad and facing north one can see the Methodist Church parsonage and Allen Ruffin Avenue that intersects with Eno Street. Using Google Earth one can zoom down on the houses bordering it. Of course, there was the parsonage, actually facing the railroad. Then there was the Weldon Riley house on the right. Moving along, the first house on the left was mine. The next house on the left is where Ed and Sadie Riley lived. Mom tells the story that Mrs. Sadie had four sons in the army in World War II: Hebron, Ralph, E.T., and Gaither. One day while looking out her kitchen window, Mom saw Mrs. Sadie rushing toward our back door. She almost fell into Mom's arms. She was trying to talk, but was unable to communicate. Mom immediately thought that one of her son's must have been injured or possibly killed in action. Mom asked her over and over what was wrong and all Mrs. Sadie could do was point to her mouth. Then realization came to fruition. The woman was choking. The Heimlich maneuver was, at that time, far in the future. Mom reacted by hitting Mrs. Sadie on her back as hard as she could. The immediate result was a large biscuit flying across our kitchen and into the sink. Mom thought if it had hit a window it would have broken it. As it turned out all of Mrs. Sadie's sons made it through the war---and she did too, thanks to my mother.

Allen Ruffin Avenue looking North. Mrs. Sadie Riley's house is visible on the left.

Growing up in West Hillsborough, I didn't know one individual of color. I do have a vague memory of playing in my front yard with a little boy named Paul who happened to be African American. I guess I was about eight and he was a little older. I remember that he was bigger than me. His Aunt Matt Tapp was doing housework for Mrs. Sadie Riley next door. After writing about that memory in the News of Orange years later, I received an email from a J.P. Alston, now living in Charlotte. He was originally from Hillsborough and either subscribed to the newspaper or had received a copy from a family member. He remarked that he had seen the article and remembered playing with a boy named Charles. We communicated over time and both realized that more than 60 years cannot erase fond memories of childhood play.

Jim and Nelia Faucette's home was next on the left. Eventually that part of the street became known as Widow's Row. By the time I was eighteen, Mrs. Primmy Riley (Weldon's wife), my mom, Mrs. Sadie, and Mrs. Faucette were shorn of their husbands. I remember swinging in a hammock during warm summer evenings listening to Dad, Mr. Jim, and Mr. Trussie Hardie as they shared yarn after yarn. One remembrance was how scared I was when they shared ghost stories from their younger days. They never knew how terrified I was while they spun those yarns. Dad told the one regarding his teenage days when he was with his girlfriend sitting on a log out in the Guilford County woods.

The moon was shining brightly and love was in the air. Suddenly, there was the sound of approaching horses. Dad said they came closer and closer. There must have been 50 or more. He peered through the moonlit night and saw absolutely nothing. He said they came so close he could smell them, and the hair was standing up on his head in terror. As quickly as they came, they were gone. Nothing was ever mentioned about the reaction of the young lady. I'm not sure if she ever went out with him after that. Would you? Jim Faucette smiled and with his southern drawl, looked at Dad and said,

"C.B. the sounds you heard were probably the rapid beats of your heart."

"Jim, Dad responded, "you don't know what fear is until you experience something very much out of our world of ordinary existence"

Then he reached back to another time, actually in the late 1800's when he was about twelve. It seems he had been visiting his brother Clay's house and left about 9:00pm. It was during the fall and it was cool enough for him to wear his old weather-beaten jacket. Of course, the worn road wasn't paved and he went by the stables near the New Garden Friend's Church adjacent to Guilford College. He remarked that it was cloudy that night; the cold breeze foretold the coming of an early winter. Suddenly, a light appeared on the side of the road. It was bright enough to illuminate the head of an old mule with its head reaching over the rail of the pasture fence. The light slowly moved to the center of the road and then stopped. There was complete silence. The mule then jumped, knocking the top rail off the fence. Dad also jumped and screamed at the same time. He must have been standing about 25 feet from the strange apparition. And then just as it had begun, the light moved slowly across the road and disappeared into the honeysuckle bushes. Dad immediately took off running and didn't stop until he breathlessly fell into the door of his home, carrying with him the scent of those honeysuckles and the realization that something uncanny had entered into his otherwise humdrum life. The next day he went back to that same place. Strangely, the mule was gone and the fence rail was intact. He looked around and didn't see any tracks, mule or otherwise. Mr. Johnson, who managed the stable, added mystery to mystery by saying that he didn't even have a mule. Go figure!

I'M SO COLD

Going back toward the railroad, one passes again the Ed and Sadie Riley house. I remember Dad telling me about Mrs. Sadie's son, Jimmy, who had been out late and had perhaps a few drams too many. His dad had been digging a septic tank, and Jimmy had inadvertently fallen into the hole. He stayed there for several hours and was crying out,

"Its cold down here!"

When daylight came, my dad heard the sad voice and rescued Jimmy. That episode was told over and over in West Hillsborough. It reminded me of the story about a gentleman who one night decided to take a short cut across the town graveyard.

The moon had disappeared behind a cloud and the young man fell headlong into an open grave. The walls were muddy and steep and he tried and tried but couldn't free himself. At about the same time, the town drunk was staggering through the same cemetery and overheard the unlucky fellow cry out,

"It's cold down here!"

He made his way over to the open grave and looked down into the darkness. Again, the trapped fellow cried out,

"It's cold down here!"

The old inebriate answered,

"No wonder you are cold; you've kicked all your cover off."

TWO TRAGIC DEATHS

From the railroad where it intersects with Allen Ruffin Avenue, one looks east toward the old Eno Mill. It is now closed and several businesses have taken up space within its labyrinth. You see the mill and the depot in the distance. Memory takes me back to the horrifying death of Russell Bivins and Sapphire Ashley. One crisp autumn morning, Mom rushed home from her third shift job, screaming as she came in the back screen door.

"The train! The train! It hit and killed Russell Bivins and Sapphire Ashley!" Before the school bus came, I had to get to the grisly scene. It was about 200 yards from home and I ran as fast as I could. Russell's body had been removed. Wrile Dollar said Russell just had a bump on his head but he was just as dead as Sapphire. Sapphire was not as fortunate in her untimely death. Funeral home people had scraped up her remains and actually shoveled them into an old tow sack. A foot had been found still enclosed in a blood-soaked shoe. I vividly remember seeing hair wrapped around bolts in the cross-ties. Somebody had tried to cover up brain remains but the coral shaped white mass could still be seen through the gravel bed. I guess I was about ten years old, and one never forgets that moment when life is snuffed out in one person and obliterated in another.

Brian Taylor, the local barber, told me years later that he had serious suspicions about the "accidental "deaths. In a few words, Brian didn't think it was an accident at all and said,

"Charles, I saw Russell and Sapphire sitting on the railroad tracks just above the overpass at the depot at about ten o'clock. They had been drinking, but I don't think either was drunk. We talked for a while and Russell said that he would see me the next day, because he needed a haircut. How was I to know that I would be the last person to see him and Sapphire alive--or was I?"

I was getting my ears lowered in the Taylor barber shop. Horace, Brian's dad was cutting my hair and Brian was trimming Otha Turner's. Brian reaffirmed his convictions by adding, "I think there was foul play."

WHAT COULD HAVE HAPPENED--FICTION BASED ON FACTS

You now know what everyone else knows about the deaths of Russell Bivins and Sapphire Ashley, but is there more?

There was a tent revival on the corner right across the road from the tracks. A year had passed and less and less talk went on about the deaths. Mom had taken me to the revival and I was mesmerized by the preacher. He was telling about God's people escaping from the old pharaoh. To emphasize the escape, he got on a straight-backed chair and literally rode that thing all across the sawdust stage. Now for an 11 year old boy that was some excitement, but nothing compared to what was to come that night. First, I had to get into trouble. When the preacher got into the boring part, at least for me, I caught sight of a large moth circling the top of the tent. Almost unconsciously, I got out of my seat and started following that moth. Would you believe, I came to my senses right at the foot of the steps leading up to the stage? That old preacher looked down at me and shouted, "Boy, God will take care of that moth! Now get back to your Mama right now!" That was embarrassing both to me and Mama. I scurried back as fast as I could to her side. She could really give some mean looks.

A roughly hewn alter was set up down at the front of the stage. After the preacher asked for money, he then gave the alter call for anyone there to be saved. Verses of "Just As I Am" drifted over West End and across the tracks to the river road. A figure, almost unnoticed on the back row, got up and took a couple of steps toward the alter. He suddenly cried out,

"I can't take it anymore. For a year now I have lived with the blood of two people on my hands. I confess to God and everybody that I killed Russell Bivins and Sapphire Ashley." I loved her. She told me that if I didn't quit drinking, she wasn't going to have nothing to do with me. I got drunk and looked out my window and saw her and Russell. I guess I just went crazy. I got a hammer out of my tool chest and crept up the side of the railroad track. I waited at the crossing. Then I heard the train coming in the distance. The noise kept them from hearing me as I slowly made my way up behind them. I hit Russell as hard as I could with the hammer. He quickly collapsed at my feet. Sapphire had fire in her eyes as she jumped toward me, screaming,
"Hiram, what have you done?"
"The ground was shaking from the oncoming train. I gave her a push and splat, her screams were lost in the sound of the blaring horn of the train as it approached the crossing. I am now confessing to God and everybody. I have been living in Hell for the past year. I pray to God that I won't have to live there for eternity."

I learned later that his name was Hiram Johnson. He was from White Cross in the southern part of Orange County, but had moved to the Monkey Bottom section of West

End. That creek-side development got its name from the carnivals that used to come through from time to time.

It just so happened that Sheriff Madrey was standing by the corner of the tent and he was as startled as anybody. He went over to Hiram, put his hand on his shoulder and quietly escorted him to his car. Was it fate that placed that revival tent near that track, or did Sheriff Madrey hope that somehow the murderer would be reached with those actions?

THE DEPOT

From the railroad crossing looking for about a quarter of a mile, one can see the overpass and the location of the former depot. Nowadays this is the entrance to Gold Park. The overpass holds a fearful memory for me. I remember riding the school bus when the teenaged driver decided to drive the bus through the wrong side of the posts holding it up. There is a sharp curve there and if something had been coming, a tragic collision could have occurred. Fortunately no one was coming and the young man just laughed and laughed. There is always a threat when one takes his life in his own hands but how helpless is the feeling when someone else takes your life in his hands?

An early memory of the depot is going with my mother to Durham for Christmas shopping. There was no car in our immediate family. In the early 1940's, there were separate waiting rooms for "whites" and "coloreds." The same was at the Durham station when we got there.

Later memories were closely tied to my newspaper route. The Durham Morning Herald was brought there about 5:00 in the morning. Buster Davis and I would meet there. He carried to one section of West Hillsborough and I had the Eno Mountain part. I remember once we got to the depot before the delivery guy got there. We climbed up on top of the depot and threw pebbles at him in the darkness. He kept looking around, shrugged his shoulders, and got in his car and drove away, never knowing it was us or where we were.

I recall a frightening school bus ride at this spot.

THE PAPER BOY

I don't remember how I got the carrier job, but it was my first work for pay. I think my half sister, Phyllis knew the delivery guy. I guess I was about 13 and I carried it until I graduated from high school. It had rained heavily the night before my first morning on the job. When crossing the Eno River bridge to the Mountain mill village, the eerie sight of the river over its banks greeted me. Reflections from the street lights illuminated the fast running waters during the early morning hours.

One morning while approaching the depot, I saw a body lying under the streetlight at the corner adjacent to the railroad station. I didn't know if the man was drunk or possibly even dead. I had to go around the figure to get to my papers. Quietly, I tiptoed to the farthest side of the street. Suddenly to my horror, the individual leaped to his feet and ran toward me.

"Good morning, Charles!" shattered the quiet as Bryant "Buster" Davis greeted a breathless me. Buster was always doing something like that. One morning it was a drunk person staggering from one side of the road to the other and just as he stumbled toward me, again I heard, "Good Morning, Charles."

The newspaper at the depot sometimes transferred scary moments from its pages to the hair on the back of my neck. One such occurrence was the headline that screamed, "Beast of Bladenboro Strikes Again." Evidently some horrendous creature was killing livestock and pets in the town of Bladenboro. Now, I didn't know where Bladenboro was and I'm still not really sure. The morning I read those headlines, it was wherever I was. Imagine taking that story with you as you walked through the early morning fog toward the Mountain mill village. I kept looking over my shoulder and becoming alert to every strange sound. Suddenly, I heard a distinct "WOOF" behind me. I turned to see the biggest dog I had ever encountered in my life. He growled again and I screamed and jumped about five feet into the air. I went one direction and the dog went the other. Looking back, he was probably more scared than I, but that was probably impossible.

Tommy Smith lived, or at least slept, in the abandoned Gem Theater in West Hillsborough. He was a boisterous, outgoing, friendly person. He was a great paper customer. I would toss the news through the crack in the door and continue my route. Timing is always important in any facet of life and getting paid by Tommy was a dilemma in orchestration. If I could reach him immediately after pay day, I was ok. He paid happily. If I missed it by a few hours his money was already invested in a weekend of heavy drinking. He still probably owes me money. My brother-in-law, Kenneth Hicks, remembered his Navy experiences and was stationed briefly in California. He saw no one he knew for months; and then one day as he was coming off his ship, he heard, "Hey, Hicks!" Lo and behold it was Tommy Smith three thousand miles from home giving him a thrill and sense of place.

Tossing the newspaper is a lost art. I'm surprised they never suggested entering the skill in the Olympic Games. Some carriers were masters of sailing that morning paper right up to the customer's door. Unfortunately, I was not one of them. The Walters house was my toughest challenge. Thelma Walters was my first love. She never knew it. She worked at the Savings and Loan and I opened my first savings account there only because she greeted me at the counter. I really wanted to get her newspaper right up to her door; however the yellowing memories of past failures were spread all over her roof top. One morning, a miracle occurred when an errant flight sailed right into an open bedroom window. Now that was service with a smile.

Across the street from the Walters' house was the home of Sallie Allison. Years after my paper carrying days were over, I wrote this tribute to her in the *News of Orange*:

"Anyone who ever rode through West Hillsborough probably saw the lady sitting on her porch in a favorite chair returning a friendly wave of her hand. I read today that "Miss Sallie" Allison, age 92 would no longer be the official greeter from her front porch or Eno United Methodist Church where you regularly found her. The paper said she died Monday, Sept. 29. The article was too short! I was Sallie Allison's paper boy many years ago. It was a joy to stop by her house on Saturdays. She had a way of making people feel good about themselves. Another blessing came my way on Sunday because many of us were fortunate to attend church with her. Years passed. Some of us moved away. When we came back for a visit, "Miss Sallie" made us feel that we hadn't really left. In a time of change, let us be thankful for people who are constant and real. Sallie Allison was such a person. Her life was an inspiration and her memory a benediction."

There were other paper boys during that period. Jack and Gene Knight delivered to Hillsborough proper (the historic part of town--referred to by a future co-teacher, Hiram Coble, as "hysteric" Hillsborough). Jim Parsley also delivered papers to downtown Hillsborough. A paper boy considered a legend in his time was Wayne "B.T" Johnson. William Parker went out one cold Sunday morning and couldn't find his paper. Across the bottom he could see Wayne in front of Butch Raynor's store throwing papers into an old burning trash barrel to keep warm. One must have been William's. One Saturday while collecting his money in the Mountain mill village, Wayne repeatedly knocked on a door. Finally he grabbed a loose board on the side of the house, pulled it back and released it with a loud "Blam!" Over and over the sound echoed across the river and around the neighborhood. He then yelled, "I know you are in there. Come out and pay me!" Someone finally came to the door--Wouldn't you?

The last day I carried the paper before leaving for college, Buster and I met at the depot at about 5:00am. I brought one half of a watermelon and he brought some Pepsis and we celebrated our time together, knowing that our paths were separating far more than just carrying the papers in different sections of town. I look back with some nostalgic sadness on that moment in time. In the 1958 SILHOUETTE Hillsboro High School yearbook, in the senior Last Will and Testament section, you will see the following: "I, Charles Bell Stanley, will to Buster Davis all of the wonderful and pleasant memories of me--that is if he should consider them as such."

West End today: The Gem Theater is no more, but one can enjoy great food at the Hillsborough BBQ Company.

THE RAILROAD RAN THROUGH US TOO

Growing up 200 yards from the railroad in West Hillsborough was instrumental in making me somewhat obsessed with trains and railroads. Early memories of troop trains and the military machines passing before my eyes took me far away. A song that still vibrates in my head sings, "In a lonely shack by a railroad track, he spent his younger days; and I guess the sound of the Outward Bound made him a slave to his wandering ways."

Standing at the rail crossing adjacent to the former C.E Riley store in West Hillsborough looking west, one can see the distant curve in the track. In my mind's eye, I can visualize walking the track and into that curve. En route to my right, I see a small park leading down to a stream. Right about there is where my dad had what he called a "wet wash laundry." It seems that he picked up laundry from the mill village, washed the clothes, and then returned them to be hung out on the lines. I think he went out of business during the Depression. Back to the railroad track. I remember standing in the middle of the curve when a freight came rumbling through –and I mean an earth-shaking, make your knees tremble and the hair stand up on the back of your neck rumble. The mighty engines and following cars seemed to tower over me. I believe the rails tilted there and you were actually beneath, and made miniscule, during the powerful experience. Then as quick as it had come, it was gone.

Sometime back in the 1950's Dad and I were watching TV one night. It was probably Channel 2 out of Greensboro or Channel 5 out of Raleigh. Actually, we were probably watching the test pattern. There was always something wrong with the transmission of those mysterious waves. Dad always tried to adjust the set, thinking he could make the test pattern go away. Suddenly, the ground began to shake and there was a loud grinding noise somewhere outside. I ran to the front door and peered out into the darkness to see fire and smell the sharp burning odor of hot metal. Dad and I were quick to realize the looming shapes of a train wreck.

There were probably 15 or 20 freight cars that had derailed and were located between Eno Methodist Church and the Cone Mill Plant. Dad and several of his friends, Trussie Hardy, Jim Faucette, and Sam Adams, set up their own camp overlooking the operation of the removal of the twisted remains. For several days, they were amazed at the work done by the cranes and other heavy equipment involved in the recovery process.

Back to the railroad, to the left of the curve where the rails tilted was a field Herley Dickey used for pitching while his sons Joe and Marvin and some more guys took turns batting. Past the curve is a small overpass leading to the old quarry where rock was dug to build Duke University. After walking over that, one is now approaching the 90-foot trestle.

WALKING TO THE 90 FOOT TRESTLE

Since there was no car in my family, there was a lot of walking. One of my favorite jaunts was to the 90 foot trestle. The railroad was about 200 yards from my home and traversing the one mile walk to the trestle was a piece of cake. The trestle spanned the Eno River and one could peer between the cross ties to the stream far below. The bridge towered over the trees. Walking the trestle always brought about a heart pounding feeling of extreme excitement. I wonder if Sir Edmund Hillary felt that way when he climbed to the top of Mt. Everest. Mom said to listen for an approaching freight and some of us guys would put ears to the summer hot rails and try to pick up the far-away whine.

I don't ever remember being on the trestle when the train came through; however, there was a much told story of Monroe Oakley's beloved milk cow, Bossy (or was it Bessie) and her ill-fated encounter.

Mr. Oakley's fence bordered the railroad and a fallen tree limb had crushed the fence and freed the curious bovine. Immediately, she stepped over the limb and plodded down to the tracks. Moments later Bossy (maybe it was Bessie or perhaps even Betsy) found herself smack dab in the middle of the 90 foot trestle. Suddenly the stillness of the night was shattered by the far-away whistle of an approaching freight train. The full moon illuminated the scene as the one-eyed monster rounded the curve and came straight at the terrified cow, frozen with fright in the middle of the trestle. The ground was shaking and Bessie (or Bossie, or Betsy, or perhaps Flossie) was bawling and the train kept on coming. At the very last second, the cow turned and plummeted off the tracks downward with a

M
  O
   O
    O
    O
    Splash!

Early the next morning, Monroe Oakley got his milk bucket and went out to find his cow. He called her by name (which one, I just don't know). He called and called but to no avail. He discovered the downed fence and immediately feared the worst. Downtrodden, he went back to his house there across from the water works. He thought he heard a "Moo!" and he felt he must have imagined it. Then he heard it again and looking out his window saw his beloved milk-maker standing in the front yard, soaking wet. The puzzle remained intact until George Dabbs who worked at the depot told Monroe that the engineer of the freight had exclaimed that he had seen a cow flying off the 90 foot trestle and further declared that he was sober at the time.

HURRICANE HAZEL

I remember Hurricane Hazel of 1954. Hurricanes were very rare visitors to Hillsborough and the surrounding area. When Hurricane Hazel hit our town, school was in session and the decisions made by local authorities by present day standards were poor to say the least. School was dismissed in the middle of the storm. Students walking home were seeing trees being ripped out of the ground by the strong winds. Riding the school bus was no less harrowing. When we reached the railroad tracks across from Betty Riley's store, the bus stopped to let several of us West Hillsborough kids off. Giovanni Crawford, a 7th grader, fainted and some of us guys carried her across the tracks to the store. When I reached home, drenched and wind-blown, I terrified my Mom who had been fast asleep--after working the third shift at the Eno Mill the night before. I don't know where Dad was. Perhaps he was still at the store playing checkers. More than 50 years later at my wife's high school reunion, I saw Giovanni Crawford and asked her if she remembered Hurricane Hazel. She quickly replied that was the scariest experience of her life. Her husband was with her and I embellished the story a little by saying a train was also coming when we carried his future wife across those tracks. He promptly thanked me for saving her life.

MOVIE TIME

There were two theaters in Hillsborough when we were youngsters. The Gem was in West Hillsborough and the Osbunn was in town. On Saturday afternoon several of us guys would walk past the depot to the theater. I remember passing Ira Peed's grocery store and the West Hillsborough Post Office. Next to the theater was a barber shop and at one time "Stinky Pyles" ran a cafe. Belleview Cotton Mill took up the rest of that locale. I remember paying nine cents to get in and watch such memorable classics as "The Thing From Another World" and Jane Russell in "The Outlaw." The first was viewed through the little slits between the seats directly in front of us. At least that was the way Gene Albright watched it. I saw the Jane Russell movie when I was about ten. Fellows who were about two years older seemed to enjoy that more than I did.

When the feature was over, we exited into the bright sunlight. I don't remember a more startling sensation than coming from darkness into that bright sun. From West Hillsborough we walked another mile to the Osbunn Theater in town to see the next movie.

I remember coming out of the theater and into the night air. There were always four or five of us guys walking all the way back home in West Hillsborough. Of course we had to take the shortcut through the old slave cemetery, holding our breaths all the while. No one would ever admit fear even though we were terrified. One night we were almost home when we heard a loud hissing noise in the pitch dark bushes just to the left of the road as we walked near the railroad tracks. Hair was standing up on the back of my neck. Suddenly the shape of a person loomed out of the shrubbery. It was James "Pud" Cole who had heard us coming and hid beside the road. We all laughed and said we knew it was him all along. Sure we did!

The Margaret Lane Cemetery is sometimes called the Old Slave Cemetery

MOTHER'S SACRIFICE

On a cool autumn evening with smoke curling out of the mill village chimneys, I distinctly remember the shrill sound of Fay Dean Summey calling her children home from play. The call of "Aaaaarthurrrrr" wafted across the railroad tracks and let me know it was also time for me to go home. I think of the sacrifices those mothers made while trying to work a full shift, rear children and provide stability to a home.

My mom, Myrtle Ray Medlin Stanley, went to work on the third shift (11pm – 7am) the day that I entered first grade. In those early years, I took her for granted and why not? When I woke up in the morning, she was there having just gotten off work. She fixed my breakfast, dressed me, and sent me off to school. When I came back home she was there, having slept during the day. When I went to bed at night, she was there to tuck me in. While I slept, she was working her night shift.

Incredible as it may seem, she continued working at the Eno plant until the day I graduated from college and then she retired. I was so glad to be able to tell her how much her sacrifices meant to me.

There were about 150 houses in the Eno Mill Village. In almost everyone there was a similar scenario. I even heard of mothers actually falling asleep at the supper table, exhausted from the daily routine. I never did like the supposed John Wayne quote, "My wife can work if she wants to as long as she has supper on the table for me at night."

I personally like to think that the whole family worked together. A lot of older children grew older even more quickly having to look after the younger ones and also help with the chores.

People moved often in the village. Mothers were always looking for a better house, perhaps one closer to work, or maybe just a change of scene. I remember knocking on the door of one of the houses thinking that my half-sister lived there. I yelled, "Open up, I know you are in there!" Then I glanced next door and saw cousins Benny and Gene Albright playing. The door swung open and I was looking at someone I didn't know. That was embarrassing, for sometimes people moved and they forgot to tell 10-year-old me.

I know that my dad helped with cooking some of the time. I distinctly remember one ill-fated meal in particular. Dad mixed up all of the ingredients for squirrel stew and put the pot on the electric stove burner. Sometime after that, he remembered he was supposed to meet Mr. John Midgett the insurance salesman at Betty Riley's store for a checker match.

His memory did not include turning off the stew. While he was gone the water gradually boiled away leaving only the squirrel and vegetables in the bottom of the pot. Dad somewhere along the way suddenly remembered and jumped up throwing checkers all over the store. He rushed home to find a hole burned in the bottom of the pot and felt fortunate that the house hadn't caught fire.

Mom awoke from her deep sleep after working the third shift and was almost overcome by the odor of the burnt squirrel. We did not have a happy household for several days afterward. I often wondered if my classmates at school could smell the stench on my clothes. I guess we were lucky to still have a house.

My mother, Myrtle Ray Medlin Stanley, with my daughter Carol in 1966

The Cone Mill Eno Plant employed 600 people working three shifts. It was central to everyone who lived in West Hillsborough. This photogragh was taken in 2018.

Pictured is Eno United Methodist Church. The Sunday School building on the left was one of the original mill houses moved from the mountain.

ENO CHURCH

One of my earliest memories of Eno Church was a painful one. Mr. Isaac Brown was mowing the church yard grass one hot summer day and I was following behind the mower. The pointed shard of a broken window pane, probably from one I had broken, pierced my bare foot. I was perhaps 6 or 7 at the time. Mr. Brown picked me up and carried me to my house which was adjacent to the church. I vividly remember the pan of water discolored with my blood as he and Mrs. Sadie Riley, a next door neighbor cleaned the wound and bandaged it up. I recall telling everyone that Mr. Brown was the doctor and Mrs. Sadie was my nurse. It's funny that I don't remember Mom or Dad being there at the time. Mr. Isaac Brown was the Sunday School superintendent. I remember him looking out over the congregation one sparse Sunday and saying, "I see many absent faces here today." Other words of wisdom was him referring to the church as his "refueling station."

One Sunday I was sitting by the open window of the church when I saw a lady leading a crying little girl from the building. I have no idea how old I was at the time. I just remember that I was the reason she was in distress. How was I to know that lady, Edith Thompson Brewer, would become my Mother-in-Law. Years later I was in one of the rear classrooms of that church when the same girl came by the window. This time she was smiling and was wearing a beautiful wedding dress. More than 50 years later, memories of Eno United Methodist Church bring both of us back home.

Charles and Lynda were married August 18, 1962

Pictured is Rev. Grill and wife Helga with their young daughter, Natalie at Homecoming several years after he served as minister. The man on the right is my wife's grandfather Herbert Thompson

Eno Church introduced me not only to my future wife but also provided a spring board toward college and beyond. The ministers of that tiny church were all Duke Divinity students. The church could not afford a full time pastor. Living next to the parsonage, I became familiar to them as a neighbor. They were my first professional role models. Since there was no car in my immediate family, Reverend Frank Grill took it upon himself to teach me how to drive.

I have a vivid memory of turning off Churton Street in downtown Hillsborough and heading directly toward a telephone pole. It was then that I heard my minister scream words I had never heard before that moment. Frank once took me to his Baltimore, Maryland childhood home. I guess that was the first time I had ever been out of North Carolina. My world had begun to grow.

Reverend Rue Wesley and wife Gen were a parsonage family when I was a senior in high school. Rue even helped coach the high school junior varsity football team. We often had neighborhood tag football games in the shadow of the church steeple. I remember James "Pud" Cole remarking,

"Charles, I really like your preacher. He cheats just like we do."
I'm sure these ministers and others were instrumental in introducing me to college. Someone paid for me to go to summer youth conferences at Duke University and Louisburg College.

Hazel Parker was the pianist at Eno Church. She performed the first music I ever heard. She was a quiet, humble lady, who made you feel special in her presence. She played at my wedding; at Dad and Mom's funerals; and of course countless other occasions. The following is a tribute to her influence on our lives.

THE GIFT OF HAZEL THOMPSON PARKER

The gift of song was for us to hear
It has been given year after year.
Hazel, you have played for fifty years
Leading Eno Church through laughter and tears.
The music flowed from the church on the hill
And touched us where we deepest feel.

For many the first Holy music we knew
Came from talent given to you.
When our children lift their voices
You had a part to play in their choices.
The music played is really you,
So gentle, harmonious, and true.
Paul said, "Love is patient and kind;
In it, arrogance you will not find."
You are a model; humble you came.
The letter "I" is not in the name
Of Hazel Thompson Parker.

"O For a Thousand Tongues" you played
And for that many you probably prayed.
I think you have them in a way.
This is Homecoming and they're here today.
There's Mrs. Mary sitting in her pew,
And Dad, Mom, and Frances, too.
There's Sara, Coy, and Isaac Brown;
Mrs. Sallie and the Kennedys who lived near town.
Mr. Herbert and Mr. Bill;
Their faith and joy we can feel.
They will always be here.

What else can we say:
We love you HAZEL THOMPSON PARKER.
God bless you on your very special day.

Hazel Parker is pictured on the front row, fifth from the left. The first ladies on the front and back row are Edith Thompson Brewer and Eloise "Sally" Oakley.

Homecoming was a special day for Eno Church. Usually a former pastor would deliver the message of the morning. Hazel Parker was a cousin to Edith Thompson Brewer (my mother-in-law) and Eloise "Sally" Oakley. At a later Homecoming, Sally and Edith received plaques in recognition for their service to their church and community.

SALLY AND EDITH

We gather here today to celebrate our past
And gain wisdom to face the coming day.
Two sisters have helped with the first and last.
So about them both we have a lot to say.

Sally, you have stood by many in their grief
And shared laughter on brighter days.
You are an example of the wonderful belief
That signifies the meaning of True Church ways.

Edith, there's something about preserving the past
That reminds us of tomatoes and beans.
Cooking, canning, and saving at last
To enjoy when a new season opens it seems.

Sally and Edith are into saving to preserve
But what they do in the end is the key.
They both give, nurture, and most of all serve
Their neighbors, church, and yes, you and me.

Sally and Edith have always been close.
Old Hill, Fairview, and now Coachwood.
They're really closer than most;
About 200 feet now and still get along good.

In a lot of families people fall out
And go for years and don't converse
I can say without any a doubt
That in their case it's actually reverse.

Sally, Edith, beloved friends to us young and old
Your devotion to your church is a great ideal.
Your warmth of welcome never seems to grow cold.
Please accept our tribute. You are true and real.

Edith and Sally lived within shouting distance in Fairiew.

Sally and Edith through the years.

During one Homecoming Sunday an entire family was honored for their many contributions to the Eno Church on the hill.

THE RILEYS

Rileys come in assorted shapes, sizes, and numbers, mostly numbers
I remember sitting in the west side Stanley-Brewer-Hicks pew
Looking across at the Riley entire east side of the church.
Everybody was there. I'm not saying that everybody was on time.
Yes, those assorted shapes, sizes, and numbers came to church. I always
Saw them there.

Many Rileys aren't called that. Some are named Wilder, Overman, or such.
Actually some like their names so much they marry Rileys so they are
Known to be called for instance Hazel Riley Riley.
Everyone around here knows a Riley. In fact most everyone is one.

A community needs a strong name and West Hillsborough is no exception.

Does prayer make a difference in the short time we have here?
If it doesn't many of us would not be sitting here today.
For I remember a beautiful prayer from Mrs. Mary Riley asking her
Father to bring all of her children into Eno Methodist Church.
Eventually they all did come and the music was sweeter and the
Re-uniting of one family made us all more aware of the promise made:
Everything you have need of will be added if you first seek His Kingdom."
Now years have passed and once again we meet on the grounds of the little
Church on the hill to share not only our food but the memories that
Eventually shaped us into who we are. Thank you Rileys for your part.

HIGH SCHOOL ATHLETICS

Did I tell you about playing sports growing up? Football and baseball. I played midget football for the Eno mill sponsored team. I guess I was about 12 years old. I played end and I remember my coach George L. Allison saying if you can touch the ball with the tip of your fingers when it is thrown to you, you can catch it. I couldn't weigh more than 115 pounds to play. We dressed in the old school building in West Hillsborough and practiced and played in the ball park down by the train depot.

When I reached 9th grade and wanted to play high school ball, my dad didn't want me to. I guess he was afraid I would get hurt. He played checkers at Betty Riley's store and Mr. John Midgett, insurance salesman, encouraged him to let me play. I always thought there were people standing in the wings helping me in future directions. I will mention others later. I went out for the team and lettered my first year. I think you had to play in half of the games to get a letter. We ninth graders played against other schools. I can only remember one game and that was with Bethel Hill. They had wires stretched across the path down to the field and it was tricky maneuvering to keep from getting garroted.

I started at right end during my 10th grade year. The other end was an all-state player by the name of Fred Owens. I scored my first touchdown catching a pass against the county rival, Chapel Hill. It proved to be the game winner. As I have mentioned before, I was a paper carrier for the Durham Morning Herald. I rushed down to the train depot to pick up my papers, excitedly going through the sports pages to see the game summary. What a disappointment: the article screamed, "Owens catches winning pass in the Hillsboro victory over Chapel Hill." At least my friends knew the truth and that helped a little. Later I was told by one of them that Fred's girlfriend who was on the school paper was going to print it there also. At least I stopped that from happening.

I hardly remember playing my junior year, maybe I had a concussion. Coach Glenn Auman approached me at the beginning of my senior year and asked if I would play halfback. What a joy that was! We had a 6-3 record and I was an All-Conference selection and honorable mention All-State. One of my highlights was the game against Northern Durham. My first cousin, Sidney Ray, was the coach for that team. We defeated them 13-7 and I scored both touch downs. Coach Fred Claytor later told me he recalled seeing Coach Ray pour a dipper of water over his own head during that game. Gee, I could hardly wait for the next family reunion.

I had the flu in the loss to Henderson that year. I remember crying while so sick in bed. I didn't feel any better when I heard we lost 7-6 and my replacement fumbled on the Henderson 5-yard line.

The last game was against Graham High School. Graham had a single wing offense. We had played against no teams with that attack. I was still weak from my bout with the flu (searching for an excuse). Graham's Don Guthrie and I were tied for the scoring lead in the conference. Harvey Reinhardt, our quarterback, threw me a pass that Guthrie intercepted and ran it back for a touchdown, winning the game and the scoring title.

Forty-five years later in a senior golf tournament, I was paired with Don Guthrie. I asked Don if he remembered our competition. It wasn't very clear to him until I pulled out the newspaper article. We had a great time reminiscing for the next 18 holes. I hardly remember the golf game.

It's interesting that the highlights of one's life are so closely entwined with moments of sadness and loss. The night I won the Most Valuable Football player award, I happily walked into my home to find my dad having a tuberculosis attack that would eventually take him away three days after my 18th birthday and three weeks before my graduation from high school.

The fleet-footed touchdown maker of the Hillsboro Wildcats at the awards night.

THE FOOTBALL FIELD BRINGS MEMORIES

Where were you during the hot months of August from 1954 – 1957? Several Hillsboro High fellows were standing in a circle around our esteemed football coach, Glenn Auman. How hot was it? I believe one could have fried an egg on the top of his shoe. Sweaty, smelly miserable, and exhausted we stood there after about two hours of intense physical trauma, better known as football practice.

We were down in the southeast corner of the field that today would have been called the wetlands. If we had been standing on the northwest portion up near the snack shack or student store we would have been scraping our cleats on the rock formation sitting just above the surface near the 10-yard line.

Perhaps you can now picture a football field that wasn't exactly level. Actually, it was in no way level and there wasn't any grass. In one of our games we would play Northern Durham. Arriving at the Northern Knight's field, we couldn't believe our eyes. There was grass everywhere. Before the game, some of us actually got down on our knees and kissed the ground. We had a great appreciation for the haves of our world.

Now where was I, Oh, it was after practice on that day in 1957. If we had "The Weather Channel" then, we would have been in a code red alert for air quality, I'm pretty sure. A dipper of cold water or a bottle of Gatorade would have been very refreshing but we had neither. It seems that during that period of high school athletic history, water was for "sissies."

Then Coach Auman spoke, "Fellows, I know you are exhausted, battered, bruised, and want to go home to supper. Somewhere in time, you will look back upon this experience of hard knocks as preparing you for the hard knocks of life."

Way down deep, some of us were thinking, "Man, it can't possibly get any worse than

this." The coach, physical education teacher, and prophet all rolled up into one was right. We were thankful for his insight and foresight. There were times when the future looked very dim; then I would think, "Nothing is as bad as those days in the sun on the Hillsboro High football field. If I could cope with that, I can cope with this."

And we did. Even on those hot days, there were moments of redemption. Quarterback Harvey Reinhardt's father drove the Long Meadow Dairy truck. I can still see that truck come around the corner and head down the hill toward the gym. Practice dismissed, we gathered what energy left and hustled to the fountain of cold cartons of chocolate milk.

Coach Glenn Auman and wife Mrs. Henrietta Auman. Coach Glenn Auman taught at HHS 1936 – 1963 and Mrs. Henrietta Auman taught at Hillsboro High School 1937 – 1963. After HHS closed in spring of 1963 both Aumans taught at Orange High School until their retirement.

I played halfback my Senior year.

1957-58 Hillsboro High Football Team

Charles Stanley

HILLSBORO HIGH

20	*Harvey Rinehardt	B	Junior	37	Robert Sechrist	G	Senior
21	*Charles Stanley	B	Senior	36	Ray Baneville	C	Senior
22	*Ray Barnes	B	Junior	35	J. W. Dickey	G	Junior
23	*Monroe Knight	B	Senior	17	Kenneth Cook	T	Junior
24	Richard Blackwelder	B	Sophomore	16	Billy Riley	C	Senior
26	Johnnie Horne	B	Senior	30	David Hines	T	Senior
27	Walter Swainey	B	Freshman	15	Marvin Teer	E	Sophomore
28	Skippie Isenhour	B	Sophomore	14	Bryant Scarlette	T	Junior
29	*Jimmie Ray	E	Sophomore	13	David Walker	G	Sophomore
39	Dannie Ray Melton	T	Senior	14	Otis White	G	Sophomore
31	*Mason Sykes	G	Senior				
38	*Eugene Kennedy	C	Junior				
32	*Gary Bateman	G	Junior				
34	*Vernon Pettey	T	Senior				
19	*Joe Dickey	E	Junior				
18	Buster Davis	E	Junior				
33	*Harry Brown	T	Senior				

*Denotes Starting Lineup

Coaches—Glenn Auman and Fred Clayton

Manager—Bennie Freeland

Every Day—Drink 3 Glasses of LONG MEADOW MILK

Offside | Illegal Position or Procedure | Illegal Motion or Shift | Delay of Game | Personal Foul | Clipping | Roughing the Kicker | Unsportsmanlike Conduct | Defensive Holding | Illegal Use of Hands and Arms | Intentional Grounding | Illeg ing Fors

1957 Football Program

Before I retired from guidance counseling at Southern Alamance High School, I worked part-time in the Young Men's Shop, a clothing store in Durham. I met a man who had grown up in Hillsborough during segregation. He was about my age. On Friday nights in the fall, I was playing football for Hillsboro High and at the same time he was playing football for Central High. He could see our lights and I could see his. We both agreed that it was a crime that we were not allowed to know or play together because of the social structure at the time.

Well what about baseball? I went out for the Hillsboro High baseball team when I was in the 9th grade. I didn't make the team and I was pretty disappointed. A man by the name of Fred Seagroves had married Betty Riley, you remember, who ran the local grocery. Fred announced when I went in there that the coach had cut the best first baseman from the team. He said that loud enough for me to hear. I don't know today if he meant it, but it did wonders for my self-concept.

I went out again my 10th grade year, but Coach Fred Claytor wanted me to pitch. I didn't think I could do it so I quit. Of course I later regretted my decision. I went out again my 11th grade year and made the team. I lettered, playing in half of the games. During the summer before my senior year I played semi-pro baseball for the Brigadoon team. I don't remember how I got involved. I only know they provided a uniform and would pick me up for practices and games. I pitched for them and did pretty good. When I reported for baseball my senior year at Hillsboro, I approached Coach Claytor and told him I would like to pitch. He retorted,

"Charles, I have been trying to get you to pitch for 3 years, and I am not going to think about it this year. I want you to play center field."

I batted over .300 for the season. I remember a "correct" newspaper article that headlined, "Stanley Stars." I had hit a homerun and two singles in that game. One memory was of going over the wall in center field and down the embankment to catch a long drive from the Chapel Hill player. When I came up the runners were rounding the bases. The umpire said it was a homerun if it went over the wall, regardless of whether I caught it or not.

There was a Dunn fellow who pitched for Southern Durham. He would pitch half of the game left handed and the other half right handed. He wasn't very good either way. So much for ambidexterity.

A couple of years later, while working during the summer for the Green Giant Company in Dayton, Washington, I was working on the same job with Phil Rigdon who had pitched for Chapel Hill High. I had always heard of him and played against him, but didn't meet him until both of us were 3,000 miles away from home.

COLLEGE

"GETTING THERE WAS HALF THE FUN AS THE NATIVE SON VENTURES OUT"

Mason Sykes and I went up to Appalachian State Teachers College and tried out for the football team during spring of our senior year. I don't ever remember filling out an application to Appalachian. Mrs. Beth Forest, my high school biology teacher, took an interest in me. I was playing baseball and wasn't thinking about college. I have jokingly commented that she applied for me and since she had dated the registrar while in school there, he admitted me. I wonder how much of that was true. Coach Glenn Auman chose some of us to help teach P.E. to a special education class. That was one of those experiences leading me to major in P.E. and Social Studies. Remember, I grew up next to the Eno Methodist Church parsonage. Usually the minister's wife was a school teacher. Even though no one in my immediate family had finished high school, I found myself surrounded by encouraging role models.

How was I able to pay for my freshman year? After high school graduation, Mr. Paul Hogan, a painting contractor, came by the house looking for my half-brother, Thomas Medlin. Thomas wasn't home, so Mr. Hogan hired me. I was probably the worst painter he had ever seen. Being left handed, I always felt I was using a right-handed brush. I liked Mr. Hogan. He started every work day with his workers gathered around him with prayer. After helping the paint crew for about 3 weeks, Mr. Hogan told me he was going to have to let me go. It seems that I was putting in more hours than anyone else on his crew and accomplishing far less. Several would be absent on Friday and more on Monday. The old question, "Do painters drink or do drinkers paint?" was evident with those guys.

I remarked earlier that my dad died a few weeks before my high school graduation. He had a little insurance money that helped me greatly during that first year. Mom was working the 3rd shift at the Eno Cotton Mill and sent me a little spending money when she could.

Mr. and Mrs. Odell Sykes, Mason's parents, took us to Appalachian State Teachers College. After we got moved into our rooms, they took us downtown and then hugged Mason goodbye. Mason was a 200 pound guard on our high school football team. As the car drove out of sight, I heard the saddest sound. Mason was not just sniffing, he was bawling. I guess I felt pretty low myself. Years later, when I was a high school guidance counselor, the director of admissions at Methodist College visited our campus. I told him the above story. He later welcomed the new freshman class, and he told them the same story in front of the Dean of Men who happened to be Mason Sykes.

Another memory of Mason happened in high school. Mason and I along with Vernon Petty were tri-captains of the 1957-1958 Hillsboro High football team. He was also an outstanding first baseman on the baseball team. We called Mason the "Baron of Buckhorn" because that is where he was from.

I spent the night at his home once. The next morning he had to slop the hogs. He was carrying a pail of pig nutrient and he called back to me, "Charles, look out for the electric fence." Suddenly he heard my scream and he turned to see that I had tripped over the wire about six inches off of the ground. I was lying face down as my trembling body was getting a good dose of juice.

I survived only to survive another painful experience before the day was over. Mason asked if I would umpire a baseball game between two men's teams from the Buckhorn-Chestnut Ridge area. A fellow was running to first base and I called him out. Suddenly I was surrounded by a large number of men with fire in their eyes. Fortunately, Mr. Odell Sykes, came to my rescue. I guess baseball out in the country was more serious than I had surmised. It probably still is today.

After graduation from Appalachian State, Mason coached soccer and tennis at Methodist College, now University, in Fayetteville. Later he became superintendent of building and grounds. He retired in 2011 after being there more than 40 years. Mason, you made Hillsborough proud and Buckhorn, too. You also made an electrifying impression on a fellow classmate.

Mason Sykes' Appalachian yearbook picture

As a freshman, I was rooming with a junior, Bobby Bean, from High Point. That should never have been allowed. We had an obnoxious hall monitor. One night Bobby and his friend Phil Hunsucker decided to roll Coke bottles down the hall after midnight. They asked me to come along. I didn't know I had a choice. Each rolled a bottle down the hall, making an awful racket. I let one go and it rolled against the hall monitor's door exploding into hundreds of pieces of glass. The next day all three of us were questioned separately by Harry Sherwood, the dorm manager. I told the truth and really caught it later from the other two. It was interesting that my sophomore year I was chosen hall monitor and got my room free. Harry said I was chosen because I had been honest with him regarding my bottle rolling escapade. Isn't life wonderful?

WESLEY FOUNDATION EXPERIENCES

While in high school, the United Methodist Youth Fellowship (UMYF) was an integral part of my adolescent years. The church provided several of us with opportunities to attend district conference sessions at Louisburg College and Duke University. Many experiences at Appalachian revolved around The Wesley Foundation, the Methodist student organization. I was fortunate to have been elected president during my junior year and also served as vice-president of the North Carolina Methodist Student Movement. A memorable experience was during my sophomore year attending the Southeastern Methodist Student conference at Lake Junaluska in the beautiful southwestern North Carolina mountains. The late 1950's and early 1960's were tumultuous times. I experienced it first-hand. The students attending the conference came from seven southern states. It was an integrated multi-racial body. The first thing we discovered was that the Lake Junaluska swimming pool was segregated. Being from a small southern town, it was my first close up and personal observation of a peaceful demonstration. When the conference was over, the pool was integrated. While at the conference, we attended the wonderful outdoor drama, "Unto These Hills." It basically portrayed the abuse and mistreatment of the Cherokee Native Americans by our government and the tragedy of the ensueing "Trail of Tears." When the play was over, as I walked up the steps of the amphitheater, there were two lighted bathroom signs: White and Colored. It dawned on me that somebody had missed the point of the dramatization we had just seen. Those two experiences were profound in the development of my perceptions of my world and those with whom I shared it.

The Dark Stranger

The man plods with true aim
Upon the winding dark street
With the ever-present misty rain
Falling endlessly at his feet.

He has come a long way
And still has far to go;
As does the thawing ground
Struggling against new snow.

He has stumbled through the ignorance
That has eternally dimmed his way.
Striving, yearning for equality,
A light to brighten his day.

He is an American citizen;
A man with education;
Of what value is it,
A stranger in his nation?

The color of his skin as he passes beneath a
Light---Black!
Now you know the meaning of his endless
Plight—Black!

We are American citizens;
Also educated men;
Yet, we scoff this brother
Because he has darker skin.

For what does he perpetually yearn?
Freedom!
How long does it take him to earn?
Freedom!

WINTER RESCUE OPERATIONS

We had a terrible winter during my sophomore year of college. National Guard helicopters were using the football field and taking supplies to families far back in the mountains. Some of the rescue attempts had disastrous results. One family was out of coal, and the helicopter dropped some to them. Unfortunately, it came through the roof, causing a greater problem. There was another story of hay being dropped to a farmer's cow, but the big heavy bale severely injured the cow which later died.

My friend Darrell Saunders answered a frantic call for volunteers to assist a family in a remote Watauga County location. The father had apparently slashed his foot while chopping kindling for his wood stove. Darrell and his friends drove a jeep as far as they could until the snow became so deep that the road was impassible. Getting out and hiking through waist deep snow the objective was finally reached. The farmer thanked the group for coming and then told them that with his six children, he could get along perfectly fine. Turning around and wading back empty handed, Darrell carried a deep feeling regarding volunteering for future endeavors.

THE PAINFUL CHRISTMAS PRANK

Darrell and I were best friends in college but never roomed together. It was just before one of our Christmas holidays, and the hustle and bustle of Justice Hall on the Appalachian State campus brought even more anticipation of the approaching vacation. Entering Darrell's room and realizing he wasn't there, gave me a brilliant idea. I crawled hastily under his bed and waited patiently for his return. The plan was to let him go to bed and then wake him up by shaking and moving his dorm bed. What a terrific way to scare the daylights out of him. I waited and I waited and I waited. Guys were walking up and down the hall, but no Darrell.

I found his old duffel bag under the bed and propped my head on it. It sure was, dark, warm, and cozy under there. My eyelids started to droop, and very slowly things began to get dark. If you haven't guessed it by now, I was going to sleep. I have no idea how long I had remained in that state, and I surely had not anticipated what happened next. Darrell came into his room and began looking for his duffel bag.

He looked in the closet; he looked behind his dresser; he looked on his bed; and then he got down on his hands and knees and looked under his bed. Shocked, he saw a body stuffed under it, and with a blood-curdling scream loud enough to wake the dead and certainly loud enough to startle the entire second floor of Justice Hall, he collapsed on the floor. I had been somewhere in dreamland when the crescendo of sound broke down whatever revelry was taking place in my sleepy mind.

The screams at first seemed far away, and then I was immersed in terror. Something dreadful was occurring. A realistic example of the "flight or fight" human reaction surged through my suddenly awakened body. Energized, I quickly reacted by attempting to jump to my feet. Unfortunately, the metal bottom of the bedsprings came into contact with my

quickly clearing head. The screaming now came from me, and suddenly the room was filled with curious onlookers from up and down the hall. Saunders now thought it was very funny. The knot on my noggin was the result of a reversal of fortune of what I thought had been a well-made plan.

Sixty years have passed. Darrell and I have both retired, and we have grandchildren who could tell you the complete story. In fact, it was shared once again during this Christmas season.

Darrell and Charles with oldest daughters DeeDee and Carol.

ICE RINK JOB

James Rae Freeland and I graduated from Hillsboro High School in 1958. During my first Christmas vacation at Appalachian State, James Rae got me a job with his dad at a new ice skating rink out near Guilford College. First though, I had to learn how to skate. After falling on my face a few times, I was glad to hear that my job would take me away from the hard, cold ice. James Sr. explained that all I had to do was pull a trailer with a large sign on the back advertising the new rink. Mr. Freeland said, "Charles, just take this around to surrounding towns to inform them about the great new recreational opportunity."

The first day I had to get used to the automatic transmission on the car pulling the trailer. Now, I bet you think that was funny, but remember, there wasn't a car in my immediate family and I had learned to drive only straight shift vehicles. I kept looking for the clutch and wanting to shift gears. I eventually figured out that I didn't have a clutch and I certainly didn't have to shift those gears.

Off I went to places I had never been before: Liberty, Swepsonville, Asheboro, and other places heretofore unknown to me. Finally it started to get dark and I realized I had no idea how to get back to the skating rink. Back in those primeval days we didn't have a GPS. Heck, I didn't even have a map. Then it really got dark. Finally I saw a Greensboro sign and was relieved to be nearing my destination. Suddenly, a gust of wind blew the huge triangular sign off of the back of the trailer. I just kept on going!
Pulling in to the ice rink parking lot, I saw a worried James Freeland Sr. He came over to the car and said, "Charles we have been concerned about you, and where is the sign?"

I sheepishly said, "James, it's lying back in the middle of Lee Street."

James calmly said, "Well, I guess we oughta go back there and get it out of the road." Later, James Rae asked if I would drive the Zamboni. I couldn't get it started. That probably saved the skating rink from total disaster.

PERCEPTION SOMETIMES ONLY REVEALS ONE DIMENSION

I find myself going down the steps of my home on Allen Ruffin Avenue in West Hillsborough. It's October 1959 and I have just come home from Appalachian State for the weekend. Walking North, I'm going to visit my pal Joe Dickey. He lives at the end of the street in a yellow cinderblock house. On the left I pass Mrs. Sadie Riley's house and wave seeing her in her rocker on the front porch. I still remember her saying she would be praying for me in college.

I pass Jim Faucette's house next and remember the boxing matches Dad and I used to watch there. There is a bottom on the right where a huge poplar tree towers above. From the road, I can hear the trickling stream where a bunch of us kids used to dam up and launch pine bark boats by breaking the dam and follow them all the way to the drain pipe under the railroad. I don't remember following my boat all the way to the Eno. Maybe I did.

The road is dusty even in October. It still is a while before it's paved. Adrian Burton's house is next on the right. He and I entered West Hillsboro Elementary at the same time. Mrs. Pruitt's house sits solitary on the left side of the road. Then I seem him. Walking down Ruffin. Headed straight toward me.

It's Earnest Medlin. I have a great respect for the Medlin family. Mom was married to Lillard Medlin and after his death she married my father, Charles B Stanley Sr. From my later research a good number of the Medlins came from Lincoln County. I think there were 13 children in Lillard's family and he was one of the younger ones. Well getting back to Earnest.

He keeps getting closer and closer. Way down deep I know what he is going to ask. Ok, it's coming. "You going to college?"

"Yes, sir."

"You playing football?"

"No, sir."

"Then, why are you going to college?"

I realized then on that cool, crisp October day that people had a specific image of me that didn't reflect the total person. Maybe we all often present one dimension to some and more of ourselves to others. So much for philosophy.

Earnest went on his way and I stood there looking down at my shoes wondering what I could have said. I could have remarked that I had a part in a Greek tragedy. I played Orestes in the play "Iphigenia in Taurus." I still have the script after all these years. I don't think that explanation would have had a real effect on Earnest. Or would it?

REFLECTIONS FROM THE HIGHWAY

"MEMORIES OF A YOUNG HITCHHIKER"

SLEEPING IN THE HEARSE

There wasn't a car in my immediate family, and Appalachian State Teacher College in Boone was about 150 miles from my hometown, Hillsboro, NC. Hillsboro is now spelled Hillsborough, and Appalachian State Teachers College is now spelled Appalachian State University.

"Thumbing" was the most economical and fastest way for me to travel. Also, an 18-year old college freshman thought he was invincible as well as immortal anyway. It never took me more than four hours to travel each way.

One of my most memorable experiences was an afternoon while returning to school. Standing along the side of the road near Greensboro, I was surprised to see a long black hearse pull over. The driver fit the stereotype of ever mortician portrayed in books, movies, and television. He was somber and of course, wore a black three piece suit.

We exchanged pleasantries and he said he was going to Boone, but had to detour through West Jefferson where a wake was taking place. He pulled up into a yard filled with cars where people were paying their individual respects. My undertaker friend said he would return momentarily and I could rest in the vehicle. In a short time, my eyelids became heavier and heavier, and soon I was sound asleep. Somewhere far away in my semi-consciousness, I was aware of people passing by.

What really aroused me was the whispering voice of an elderly lady who said to her companion, "I thought he was supposed to ride in the back." She may have been surprised when I sat up quickly and smiled broadly. Mr. Mortician soon came out of the house and we continued on to Boone.

I always wondered if it really would have been more comfortable if I had been in the back. I would certainly have been even more surprising to the lady had I sat up from that location in the hearse.

1959, THE ADVENTURE BEGINS

Five of us were to meet at Charlie Guy's house on Sunday evening. I hitchhiked the 100 miles from Hillsborough to Statesville. Mom had told me it was ridiculous to go 3000 miles for a summer job, but you just couldn't tell a college freshman what to do.

After arriving at Charlie's, I turned in early. During the night I was awakened on several occasions by conversations such as,

"Joe, don't leave. Stay here, and I'll date you every night this summer." A young voice replied,

"Okay, Mary June, I'll stay." And,

"Tom, your daddy can get you on in the mill. Don't go traipsing way off to Washington state and the Green Giant Company."

"Alright Mom, I'll stay."

When Mrs. Guy called us to breakfast, there was a glum Charlie who said that we were the only two left. We struck out – Charlie did all of the driving. We slept in cheap motels at night, and I paid half of the gas and oil. The trip out cost me $60 and took six days.

While working in the cannery, I ran into a fellow from Lincolnton, NC, Jerry Aiken. We became pals and when the pea season was over, we stayed an extra week with a clean-up detail. Charlie drove out to Seattle with Jacob Koontz to visit his sister, whom he had not seen in several years. Jerry and I hitchhiked the 300 miles planning to meet up with him. Upon arriving in Seattle, we called and got no answer. Charlie had told us that they may be camping and for us to go on to the house. A cab driver said that it was $7 for a trip across town. Jerry said, "You know, Charles, I bet we could hitchhike all the way back to North Carolina cheaper than paying cab fare across Seattle."

I replied that if he was crazy enough to try it, I guess I was too. We took a bus to the outskirts of the city to a place called Parker Crossroads. I'll never forget it because I thought it was a town, but it turned out to really be just a cross road.

Rolling up in our blankets, we were soon asleep. Somewhere in my mind an alarm went off! The ground began shaking as a huge bright eye plummeted toward us out of the darkness. Shaking cobwebs from our brains, we became cognizant that we were lying ten feet from the railroad track. Little were we to know that this was an omen.

Morning came. Our very first ride was with a man in a pick-up truck who said that if somebody wanted to travel far and cheap, the best way was by a freight train. He took us to the railroad yards in Spokane and said that the Great Northern Railroad did not heavily enforce hobo regulations. He said something about a lady owned this railroad during the Depression and she had said, "Let my boys ride."

A brakeman pointed out a train that was headed for Saint Paul, Minnesota, and told us when it would be leaving. We couldn't find an empty boxcar, so we had to settle on a gondola. You've seen the kind that carries scrap metal and so on.

We ran over to a nearby café, where we got a jug of water, two packs of peanuts, and two doughnuts. Pulling out that night was about the most exciting event of my young life. Trains go places where people don't. Waking up in the night with the air rushing past your face; listening to the clickity clack of the rails; and seeing a forest fire flickering far in the distance are memories etched in my mind. Daylight came with water all around. The track followed a huge river for miles. Towns like White Fish, Montana came and went. It was August and I've never been colder than when we went through Glacier National Park. Snow was everywhere.

After three days we were exhausted, dirty, and generally miserable. The train slowed as it approached a small town. One of the bums, perhaps I should say "other bums" said we were coming to Minot, North Dakota and would stop six miles on the other side of town. Jerry said he wasn't going to ride any further, so with that, he threw his old tattered bag over the side of the now slow-moving freight and leaped out of view to the ground below.

Now, I had my good "Appalachian State Teachers College" suitcase, and I wasn't about to throw it. I jumped, but the weight of my case pulled me backward into the cinders, and everything went black.

Somewhere far away someone was yelling, "Charles, are you ok? Speak to me!" As I came to, I realized the voice belonged to Jerry. My suitcase was alright, but I had a knot on the back of my head. We made our way to the Salvation Army, where they let us change clothes, shower, and gave us free tickets for a meal and lodging at a cheap, but clean, hotel near the tracks for the night.

After recuperating, we resumed our trek – this time thumbing. In all it took six days. By the way, it did cost a little more than the $7 cab fare. It cost me $9 to cover 3,000 miles.

WORKING IN THE GREEN GIANT CANNERY

The Green Giant Personnel Office in Dayton, Washington was a low brick building with the morning sun illuminating the concrete sidewalk. When I got to the front of the line, Mr. Kitterman told me about the different job openings. I chose the one called "dumper." For some reason that sounded interesting. I was soon to find out. The peas were brought into the plant on huge trucks. Pallets with about 50 boxes of peas were stacked evenly. A forklift driver hefted them off and placed them in front of a hopper where the dumper turned and lifted each 20 pound box and emptied it into the hopper. A conveyer belt then took the peas into the bowels of the cannery. For 12 hours a night, I lifted the boxes over and over again. I remember at the end of the summer when I returned to college that some of my friends asked me if I had been lifting weights over the summer. The platform was covered but really outside the plant. I spent many a night looking up at the moon and singing, "Carolina moon, keep shining. Shining on the one who waits for me."

After the 12 hour shift, guys returned to the fence-enclosed cabins just outside the perimeter of the plant. Someone said that during World War II, it was a detention area where Japanese-Americans were interred. Each cabin had four sets of bunk beds with lockers between each. There was no insulation which led to some pretty chilly nights. There was a laundry and community bath facilities in a building out back of the cabins. A canteen where you could get hot meals was located at the cannery.

When the weather got really warm, I remember taking a blanket and climbing the bluff overlooking the town of Dayton and directly over the park with the swimming pool below. I unrolled my blanket, and slept during the day. I don't remember anyone else doing that and frankly don't remember why I did it other than just looking at it as another type of adventure.

Dayton Washington as viewed from the bluff

One summer I arrived to the Green Giant Cannery before it opened for the season. Someone suggested that I assist a local farmer in cutting asparagus. I thought, "This will be a piece of cake." Riding in the back of his pick-up, I saw this expanse of land with asparagus growing in long, straight rows as far as the eye could see. He gave me a knife that looked kind of like a putty knife with a sharp end. The only thing I had to do was put a bag around my neck, bend over and cut the asparagus. When the bag was filled, I would empty it into a hopper along the field. There was a little Latino kid starting in the row next to me. I bent over and started cutting away. When I finally filled up my bag, I painfully straightened up and realized the little fellow was almost out of sight down his row. I guess everything has to be learned and this was not in my skill set. The next day, someone asked if I were going back and I graciously declined.

The next opportunity moved me into the cannery where the asparagus canning process was going on. They gave me a job at what they called "the idiot wheel." I soon found out why it was so aptly named. The asparagus came down the chute onto a rotating, wheel-like apparatus with holes in it. Underneath, were the cans. I was given a mallet to mash the asparagus into the cans as it went round and round. When I looked up at the ceiling, I noticed that it was also going round and round and round – therefore the realization of why it was called the idiot wheel.

Another summer I rode out with Jerry Ritchie from China Grove. When the pea season was over, someone suggested picking apples in Oregon. I think we did that one day, at least long enough to get a tank of gas. Then, someone suggested we go to San Francisco to work in the soup canneries. We arrived there on the Fourth of July. Of course, none of the companies were open. Last, someone suggested we work in the wheat fields in Kansas. When Jerry's car turned toward the East Coast, no one mentioned working again. We drove all the way through Kansas and the word wheat was never uttered.

That was the summer that Lynda had told me not to come back across the Mississippi River unless I had her an engagement ring. When I got to the Mississippi, I called her and asked if I could come across. I sure didn't have enough money to buy what she wanted because my pay was sent home all summer long. I was very thankful that she assented. Things were beginning to look up. They still are today.

1960 – THE GREAT FOREST FIRE ADVENTURE

"Find him. You just gotta find him. He don't know his way in these woods!" The old man in his faded, ragged jeans grabbed the ranger by his jacket and finally got a response.

"Okay, Grasma, it's dark out there, but we will try to find him."

The Green Giant Company in Dayton, Washington closed early that summer. It rained. I worked all four summers there during my college days, and this was the only time I saw it rain. It rained on those tender peapods, and when the sun came out, they were literally broiled in the shell. One could look for miles in every direction and see dead brown pea vines.

Someone said once, "When a door closes another one opens." I was also aware that one never knows exactly what is behind the next door. The rain storms that burned the peas started forest fires in nearby Umatilla National Forest. My traveling companion, Richard Fogleman, and I saw the notice on the cannery bulletin board, "Firefighters needed!" We gathered information that a bus would be leaving at 2:00am (never knew why that time of day) to go to the forest. We were to return daily. Richard and I rented a room, and later that evening we went to the bus. Field workers had received their severance pay, and by that time many were drunk and thought the bus was the one going to Walla Walla. It was a truly sobering experience for them and also for Richard and me. We came back ten days later.

Picture an isolated ranger station in the middle of nowhere. The gray wooden structure with surrounding sheds and barns was located in the bowl of a little valley. The advent of the fire-fighters made it a noisy bustling environment. Richard and I were given 50 pound tanks of water strapped to our backs and taken out to fight "hot spots." Looking back, we could not have been given more dangerous positions. Picture the fire in one area, and sparks flying ahead and starting small fires in the distance. We came close to the fire and one never forgets seeing a tall, majestic fir tree explode with the fury of a hellacious inferno. The smoke and the heat were almost unbearable. After doing this all day, we were picked up and taken back to camp. We were given sleeping bags and immediately succumbed to the 13 hours of fatigue. Waking up the next day, I heard an old derelict, Jim Grasma, laugh and say a bear woke him licking his face.

The second day was much like the first, except Richard developed blisters on his feet and the team leader took him back to camp. I worked and worried all day about him. Would they send him back to town? Was he more injured than I thought? That evening when I straggled back to camp, there was Richard lying under a spruce tree with chipmunks playing all around him. He had gotten a job in the kitchen, and to think I had been worried about him. By the way, the food was awesome. The Forest Service took care of us really well.

Rumors were circulating that three prisoners who were fighting the fire, had been trapped in the path of the fire and were killed. They were working hot spots. Somehow, the following day, I got separated from other members of my crew. I could hear them yelling on an adjacent hillside and when I got there, they had moved on. This went on all day, and it began to get dark. Little did I know that the men had been pulled back and returned to camp. Jim Grasma was the first to realize that I was missing, and he approached the lead ranger and expressed his anguish. The ranger got a crew, and they came into the smoke-filled hellish realm of night and blew the horn on the truck. I could hear the sound in the distance and struggled through the underbrush, startling a huge deer that jumped up right in front of me, startling me in return. I was overjoyed at being found and later found out how lucky I had really been. The wind picked up that night, and the fire briefly grew out of control in the same area where I had been lost.

Jim Grasma was one of those winos who had taken the bus by mistake. Someone said that one could probably find him lying in a gutter in Walla Walla today. There will always be a place in my heart for that grizzled old fellow who wouldn't let the others forget about a young guy lost in the woods.

The forest station in Umatilla National Forest

THE ANTAGONISTIC INVITATION

Somewhere in Colorado, Richard Fogleman and I were gazing far into the distance wondering when the next car would come our way. We heard it before it came into our vision. An old dilapidated coupe inched its way to the side of the road. The car seemed to be full of people. The rear window was down and a big, husky guy pumping his ham-sized arm up and down was muttering. "Do you want to fight? Do you sons of bitches want to fight?" A very sweet-faced grandmother-type lady rolled the driver's side window down and said, "Would you guys like a ride?" The only reply I could give came, "Ma'am, I believe you have enough company already. Thank you anyway." The car eased its way back into the highway, and the last sound I heard was, "Do you want to fight? Do you sons of bitches want to fight?" I always wondered just what was going on there. It was just one of many hitchhiking experiences that I will never forget. Gee, that was more than 60 years ago.

THE "MY NAME IS CHARLES STANLEY" EXPERIENCES

Would you believe that I have been picked up three times by people whose name was the same as mine? The first was the most memorable. I was trying to get through Charlotte and back home after a summer of work at the Green Giant company in Washington State. It was one of those "could fry an egg on the highway" days. I was relieved when a car stopped ahead of me and backed up. I ran, opened the back door, threw in my travel bag, and climbed in the front seat. I thanked the driver, a middle aged, well-dressed man, and then he introduced himself to me, "I am Charles Stanley and what is your name, young man?" You should have seen the surprised look on his face when I smiled and replied, "My name is Charles Stanley, too." We traveled about two blocks when he pulled over and let me out without saying a word.

THE PROMISES TO GOD

Richard Fogleman and I were thumbing through Utah when a fellow with a beer in his lap offered us a ride. Now, I was skeptical about riding with someone drinking, but this man had his young daughter with him and I thought incorrectly that this would be okay. I don't think he ever got under 90 miles an hour, and it was dark. I prayed, "Lord, when I die, I would rather die in the daylight. Help me get through this and I will change my ways." I could imagine the plummeting car being wrapped around a tree or a bridge abutment. I can't remember just how the experience ended, but since I am still here, I guess it was okay. Oh, I have made so many promises with divine intentions tied to them. I sure remember them and I'm certain He does too.

THE "HIT YOU IN YOUR FACE" EXPERIENCE

It was a cool day in early June when I left Hillsborough en route to Charlotte to get up with Richard Fogleman to begin our trek "Out West" together. Somewhere around High Point, I got a ride with a fellow in the military. I was already skeptical about riding with someone drinking. The soldier had been drinking rather heavily I gathered, because he asked if I would drive. He soon fell asleep as I made my way toward the Charlotte destination. After about 50 miles, he suddenly woke up and looked defiantly at me and yelled, "What the big idea? What's going on here?" Startled, I asked him what was his problem. That's when he angrily said, "You've turned the car around, and you're headed the wrong way." He wouldn't listen to me and shouted, "I ought to hit you in your face!" Easing the car into a service station, I called an attendant over and said, "Could you please tell me if we are headed toward Charlotte?" He grinned and said, "Yes, you are on the correct road." My passenger looked at me and said with a sneer, "You wise ass." He then promptly went back to sleep. When I got to Charlotte, I slowly drove off the road, stopped the car, and got my travel bag. I quietly closed the door and took a couple of steps when the soldier woke up. "Where are you going? You can't leave me here!" I never looked back, but hurried into the busy downtown section of North Carolina's largest city. And to think I was still going to hitchhike at least 3000 miles that summer.

Richard Fogleman's Appalachian yearbook picture. He was a great hitchhiking companion

I haven't shared that Richard first went out west with me on my second cross country journey. I had a job at the cannery at the end of the 3,000 mile trek, but Richard did not He had assumed that if he had traveled that far that he would be given a job. He wasn't.

Years later as a guidance counselor at Southern Alamance High School, I used Richard as an example when talking to students about job searches. When Richard was told that he didn't have a job, he sat down in front of the employment office and played Solitaire. Administrative people had to walk over or around him all day to get into the building. Later, I saw him running up the road toward the workers' cabins. He shouted, "I got a job! I got a job! I'm driving a swather. What the heck is a swather?" Persistence is an attribute while in the job search.

You should have seen him at the end of his first work day. The swather cut the peas. He was covered in dirt and dust. When he took off his glasses there were just white circles around his eyes. When he took off his work clothes and beat them against the cabin, it looked like smoke from a fire. But he got a job and he was very happy.

During the forest fire adventure that I have told you about, Richard was relegated to kitchen duty due to his blisters. He confided in me that he took a bath in one of the cooking vats and couldn't remember if he had cleaned it out afterward. He said that I had remarked that it was the best macaroni and cheese that I had ever eaten. I will always wonder if the was true or was he pulling my leg?

Another interesting thing that happened during the forest fire adventure was a great theological discussion that I stumbled into in the middle of a clearing. The crew chief and a towering, powerful fellow named Luther were discussing the Bible. Luther turned to me and said, "Tell John here that everything in the Bible is true."

Okay so the 19-year old rising college sophomore was to expound upon what people for centuries had been debating. Being the wise fool (that's what sophomore means), I replied, "Well Luther, since people aren't perfect and the Bible was written by people, it probably isn't all true."

Luther turned to me, and with a great sigh, said, "And you are from the South."

Many years have passed and I wish I had only added, "Man does make mistakes, but those men were inspired by a power much greater than they were; the truths that emerged were true then and are true today."

After battling the forest fire, we approached the chief ranger to get our pay. He regrettably informed us that our money would be mailed to us.

Luther took one look at him and said, "If you don't pay these men now I'm going home with you after work tonight and stay there."

Guess what? We all got paid on the spot. The last time I saw Luther, he was walking down the railroad tracks toward Walla Walla with two chipmunks in a crude wire cage, taking them eventually to his children in Chicago.

HOTDOG ON THE HIGHWAY

I returned to Hillsborough as a young adult married to my high school sweetheart and with my young daughter Carol. Adventures from the road did not end.

Kids were coming from everywhere while I was looking out of my picture window at my home in the Colonial Hills division in Hillsborough. Our house was located adjacent to Interstate 85. There was an old song about the railroad running through the middle of the house. In my case, it was the highway.

The kids were all shouting and pointing to something out on the highway. Partially hidden behind the trees, it looked like a truck had broken down with the middle almost touching the ground. Daughter Carol practically fell in the door exclaiming, "Dad it's the Oscar Meyer wiener mobile!" We lived in that house for 13 years and only once did someone from the highway approach us for assistance. Well, this was the once. The driver knocked on my door and asked if he could use our phone. This was a few years before the cell phone era. We ushered the somewhat exasperated gentleman in and offered him some iced tea. He thanked us for our hospitality and then went to the phone.

The communicated conversation was one that has lingered with me since that late 1960's day. While calling for mechanical assistance, the person on the other end of the line asked the questions that each of us would have had we been in his position, "Could you give me a description of your vehicle so that I can send someone out to assist you?"

The driver promptly replied, "You can't miss it. It's a 40-foot-long hot dog." Way down deep I wanted to ask, "Wouldn't it have gone all the way without onions?"

The last time that I saw the intriguing vehicle, we were in the parking lot of the Grand Ole Opry in Nashville, Tennessee. Carol was a teenager and asked if I still remembered the Colonial Hills hotdog experience. Some things you never forget.

The Oscar Meyer Weiner Mobile has a spot on our Christmas Tree.

THE RETURN WEST

For years I wanted to retrace my hitchhiking path back to Washington State. In 2007, with a van loaded with daughters, Carol and Laura, grandsons Nicholas and Lucas, Lynda, me--and a giant stuffed rainbow trout that Nicholas insisted that we carry along, we launched a 21 day safari across the USA. I had waited 40+ years and would have gone earlier, but Lynda did not want to hitchhike. The trip was awesome: crossing the majestic Mississippi, riding a buckboard through a "real" Oklahoma ranch, viewing the giant meteor crater in Arizona, sweating in the Petrified Forest. I recall being amazed at the Oregon Trail wagon ruts visible in Guernsey, Wyoming. Being with my own family gave me a greater respect and appreciation for the families who traveled west in search of their dreams.

The many wagons passing through this portion of the Oregon Trail created permanent reminders of westward expansion.

We took a train from Williams, Arizona to the Grand Canyon, meandered up the California Coast, and drove the van through a tree in Redwood National Park along the way.

I will never forget watching the two boys playing in the snow at Crater Lake National Park in Oregon in June. Farther north, Seattle brought me back years ago to the beginning of my first trans-America hitchhiking experience. Climbing the Space Needle reminded me that I had done that in 1962 during the World's Fair. I had always embellished the story by saying I was the first person to climb it.

The most important stop was returning to Dayton, Washington where I had worked every summer while I was in college. Amazingly after 45 years the building was still there, although inoperative. I still remembered the sign in the employment office that read, "Both English and Southern Spoken here." The Green Giant Company paid around $600 for one month of work which also happened to be the price of one year of tuition at Appalachian State Teachers' College.

The next part of the trip was Yellowstone National Park where we enjoyed Old Faithful. Daughter, Carol, had made several excursions to Yellowstone and describes herself as a "Geyser Gazer."

An exciting experience happened while stopping on the roadside. A herd of bison came over a hill and passed on both sides of our vehicle. One could have reached out and touched them.

The final leg was our return home. I am always drawn back to memories of Occoneechee Mountain. My heart is rooted in West Hillsborough. I am thankful that my Creator provided a way for my path to encompass the wonders of His natural world and to meet the amazing personalities along the trail.

FAST FORWARD TO THE PRESENT

Earlier in this narrative, I referred to the top of Occoneechee Mountain as a place I could observe the origins of the seven decades of life on this planet, mine that is. In early spring of 2010, the Occoneechee Mountain State Natural Area sponsored a geological hike. Grandson Nicholas, and his mother, Laura, accompanied me on that warm Saturday morning. The geologist was very informative in pointing out the pyrophyllite outcrops along the trail. He explained that was the reason for the now sheer cliff overlooking the Eno River. The mineral was mined in the early 1920's and was used to make fire-proof brick for furnaces. He remarked that some was incorporated onto the nose cone of the NASA space shuttle. It is a rare mineral found in few places on earth. Okay, back to the story. After following the professor down the old path on the south side of the precipice, we left the group and climbed up the very steep north side. Laura was concerned about me because I had a defibrillator implant to assist with controlling atrial fibrillation. About

halfway up, I remembered that there is now a path with steps leading up to the top; however I wasn't going to turn around and go back down to find it. Upon reaching the top and looking across the West Hillsborough landscape, I could see the home in which I grew up; Eno United Methodist Church where I was married; Betty Riley's store; the location of my elementary school; and of course the railroad. Suddenly I felt a blow to my chest and my knees buckled! Someone said as you are dying, your life passes before you. Actually, before me in a wonderful wide vista, the places of the first years of my life literally appeared. Later I found out that my pulse rate had risen to an alarming rate and the defibrillator shocked my heart back to normal. You could imagine how Laura and Nicholas felt when I screamed.

Grandson Nicholas and I reach the top of Occoneechee Mountain

GRANDPA, PLEASE TELL THAT STORY MANY TIMES

When I was about six years old, living behind Eno Methodist Church, Momma sent me to Betty Riley's store to get some butter. There was a little path behind the church which continued toward the store. As I turned the corner of the church I saw a group of men, probably 4 or 5, sitting on crates outside Paul Riley's fish market. I had to pass right by them. As I got closer I could tell they were laughing and talking. Just as I came by them, I heard a harsh sound, "Come here boy." I walked over and I think it was one of the Adams brothers who said, "Boy, I'm going to cut your ears off." I turned and ran as fast as I could to Betty Riley's store. You know, I don't remember getting the butter, because I knew I had to go back past that group. When I finally got up my nerve, I walked back, but this time I distanced myself by walking on the far side of the road across from the store. I will never forget the laughter from those men. Suddenly I heard, "Come back here, boy. I'm going to cut your ears off now." I ran so fast I could feel the wind rushing past the ears that I hoped to keep. I don't remember what happened when I got home, but after 70 years I can still hear the voice of the Adams man, "Come here, boy. I'm going to cut your ears off."

THE SCREAMING SKULL

My grandsons, Nicholas and Lucas, and I were hiking along the mossy trail wedged between the Eno River and a rocky outcrop beneath the sheer quarry cliffs of the Occoneechee Mountain. Some are hesitant to call the Occoneechee a mountain because it's only 700 feet above sea level; however, it is believed to be the highest elevation between Greensboro and the North Carolina coast.

Nicholas asked about the occasional recesses at intervals on the narrow trail. I explained, "They were made by the cross-ties of the narrow gauge railroad that carried the quarry stone away. This is the very place that gave birth to the legend of the 'Screaming Skull' that my mother shared with me long ago." The three of us sat with our feet dangling off the path as I told the story.

In the years before the Civil War, local prisoners were used to carry out the shale-like ore that was used to pack both old and new railway beds. Rivulets of water streamed down the bare rock and soaked the ground along the ore train tracks. James Larkin, a young prisoner from Cedar Grove, was getting ready to finish a long day as the last load of ore was coming out. His old shoes that were shorn of tread suddenly slipped sideways, throwing the unfortunate James head-first beneath the oncoming grinding wheels of the ore cart. With strength coming only from a basic will to survive, the young man dug his fingers into the wet soil with a superhuman effort to extricate himself from sure death. Tragically, the heavy wheels severed his head just below the larynx or voice box. Horrified witnesses above the rails were stunned to hear, "Oh no! Oh no!" shrieking from the head as it bounced forehead over chin, forehead over chin, landing with a splash in the rushing river. The sound echoed again and again through the river valley while the bodily remains near the track still lay quivering, much like the chickens after Dad chopped off their heads for Sunday dinners past.

The Hundred Year Flood of 1908 washed out the railroad trestle near the coon rock, thus ending the mining on this spur of the Occoneechee. Years later, my mother remembered one summer night sitting in the swing on the porch of the mill village house and seeing a sight that remained with her to her death bed. As the moon leisurely meandered from a cloud bank, a figure ambled through the foggy river bottom lined with beech trees. She watched in horror as it turned to reveal only a stump where there should have been a head. Further up the stream, she heard a blood-curdling, "Oh no! Oh no!" The ghastly figure suddenly turned and stumbled toward the sound splitting screams, tripping and falling in the underbrush.

Other villagers from time to time have watched the eerie scene unfold again and again.Maybe, somewhere in a not too distant future, a mortal person will have the courage to lead the body of James Larkin to the screaming skull of the Occoneechee Mountain, and the nightmare will end for him and for you and for me.

THE SCREAMING SKULL----PART 2

There is a tale about the finding of James Larkin's long-missing head. Orville McKaskill was walking along the banks of the Eno when he was startled to see a strange white rock protruding just out of the water near the mountain swimming hole. When he looked closer, his hair started sticking up on the back of his neck, and goose bumps rippled up and down his arms. That was no rock! It was a skull. Now Orville like everyone else from the old mill hill knew about the lost head of James Larkin. He reached up and broke off an old dead branch from a sycamore tree. Trolling it through the water, Orville hooked the branch on a long vacant eye socket, and then brought it slowly to the bank.

Now I don't know what you would have done, but Orville hurried home with his newly prized possession, and promptly hid it under his bed. Jim Cole was his best friend and lived next door. He wasn't home because he had a first shift job at the Cone Mill plant. Orville could hardly wait for him to come home. Jim would help him decide what to do with his ghastly find. Finally, the 3:00 whistle blew and shortly after, Jim pulled into his driveway. He had been driving for about a year. Orville rushed out of his house and bombarded Jim,

"Betcha can't guess what I've got. You'll never guess in a million years."
Jim urged him to get to the point. When Orville revealed his secret, Jim right away told him what to do.

"Orville, we've gotta take that skull to James Larkin's grave!"
That night about midnight, Orville fought sleep but drifted off anyway. Something brought him wide awake. A faint murmuring came from beneath his bed frame. Very softly, the sound of "Help me!" came from that tow sack that held that awful find. Jumping up, Orville remembered that he was supposed to meet Jim. He crawled out his window with the sack in hand. Luckily, no parents heard them as they slowly drove out of the yard. James Larkin was buried in the Cedar Grove Methodist Church cemetery. Folks said the grave didn't have a head stone, just a marker where his body was interred. Of course, there was no need for a "head" stone--was there?

The moon was so bright and reflected off each tombstone in the old graveyard. It was almost like daylight. Both boys wondered if it would have been more scary on a darker night. This was bad enough they agreed. Orville crept up to the grave with the tow sack. He slowly extricated the hollow eyed remains from it and laid it right at the place where the thought James Larkin might be. Jim and Orville stepped back and realized their job was done. Suddenly, there was a deep trembling of the earth as the grass covered entombment lurched and buckled. Mesmerized, both boys suddenly saw two gnarled skeletal hands reaching upward and wrapping around the old skull. Just as quickly as the hands appeared, they returned to the eerie depths with what they were seeking. Somewhere far below a voice spoke distinctly and plainly, "Thank you."

THE THREE LEGGED PIG

Some time ago I was driving through Swepsonville in Alamance County. Do you know the steep hill coming down toward the Haw River from the old Quarry Hills Country Club? That's when I first saw it. I couldn't believe my eyes when just before getting to the stop sign a good-sized pig hobbled across the road in front of me. It was hobbling because it only had three legs. It went behind me and I could see in the rear view mirror as it went up the ramp to an old mill house, and disappeared through the open screen door on the porch. Sitting in an old rocking chair, there was a fellow the pig had to walk right by. My curiosity got the better of me so I parked the car in the driveway next to the clapboard house. I introduced myself to the occupant of the rocking chair and he welcomed me to join him in another rocker.

"Mister, Did I just see a three legged pig go into your house?"

"You sure did. That is the most wonderful animal in the world."

"Would you tell me why it only has three legs?" I asked.

"If you have a while, let me tell you a story…

About a year ago, my wife and two children were sound asleep when for some reason a fire started. It could have been some grease left on the stove. I don't rightly know. But anyway, as I said, we were sleeping and suddenly I was overcome by the smoke and so terrified that I couldn't even find the door. Outside, I could hear a grunting sound which helped me find the door. Just as I opened it, this pig showed me how to crawl under the smoke. I got my family and followed the pig outside. I could then hear the sirens as the Swepsonville fire department appeared on the scene, and somehow had the fire out in minutes.

"So that's what happened" I inquired. "The pig got burned and lost his leg?"

"No sir. That is not the reason."

"Well tell me more."

"Some time ago, we were visiting my family farm over in Kimesville. We have a few cows and a mean and I really mean, mean old bull. It was Valentine's Day and my young daughter was wearing a bright red dress. I turned away for a second and heard the old bull bellow. Shocked at the sound, I turned to see that my daughter had crawled under the fence and was toddling toward the snorting, pawing beast. I was frozen with fear as it charged. It all seemed to happen in slow motion: my daughter running and the bull bearing down on her. All at once there was something else in the picture. The pig came out of nowhere, grabbed that red dress, and dragged my screaming little girl under the fence to safety."

"So that was it. The pig got gored by the bull and lost his leg. Isn't that right?" I inquired.

"Nope, wrong again, my friend. Listen to the rest of my story.

My little boy had just learned to walk. We had one of those expandable barriers set up so he wouldn't fall down the steps. I went out on the porch and to my dismay, the barrier had been opened and my son was gone. My heart leaped into my throat when I heard the screeching brakes. If it had been you, you could never have stopped your car in time to avoid hitting my child, and the same thing happened to that poor driver. I actually saw him throw his hands over his eyes. To everyone's amazement, out of nowhere, came that pig again and plunged into my boy knocking him plum out of the road."

"Surely, you have now told me the conclusion of the story", I said. "The pig was hit by the car and his leg had to be amputated. Thank you for telling me about that harrowing experience."

"Sir, I am so glad you came by, but that is not what happened to that super swine. You see, the pig has been so wonderful to my family, that we couldn't just eat all of it at one time. Come back and visit, my friend"

BICYCLES MEAN FREEDOM

While sitting by my computer one morning a few years ago, I looked out the window and saw grandsons Nicholas and Lucas riding their bikes around our house. They live across the street. It was 7:15am and I thought that was pretty early to be riding before going to school. I wondered if I ever rode my bike that early in the morning. Then some early riding adventures came to mind.

My worst Christmas Day in memory was a white one. Imagine getting the greatest present Santa could possibly have brought – a brand new bike. I was devastated that he just had to have snow on the ground so the reindeer could easily pull the sleigh. You know, we seldom have white Christmases. I never could figure why the sleigh needed skids if the reindeer could fly.

Well anyway, I can still picture sitting on our screened in back porch looking out at Eno Church in the middle of a whiteout. The church was white, our house was white, and three feet of white fluffy misery came between extreme happiness and deep depression. I was sitting on that bike and riding all over the neighborhood in my mind. After seeming like an eternity, the snow finally departed.

I don't know why I had such a big bike. Maybe I was just a little kid. To get on it, I learned up against a bank between Sadie Riley's and Jim Faucette's houses. I got up on the bank and sort of halfway leaped from it to the seat of the bike. You know, like Hopalong Cassidy did on his horse Topper. The main problem with that effort was that Topper had four legs and my bike only two wheels. Talk about skinned shins and a bruised ego. Finally, I had broken in my steed and immediately named it Silver, even though it was red. I'm sure that Clayton Moore of Lone Ranger fame would have been proud. I wonder if my West Hillsborough neighbors questioned my sanity when they saw me flashing down West Hill Avenue, by Coland Riley's store, toward the railroad track shouting at the top of my lungs, "Hi ho, Silver, away!

When I was in the seventh grade I rode my bike the two miles to school. During free time after lunch, while playing on the rocky outcrop near where the new gym now stands, I fell head over heels down the steep embankment. Stunned and in pain, I came to the realization that I had torn a big hole in the knee of my new jeans that Mom had just bought me in Durham. Then I saw the real damage. My knee was badly cut from the sharp rocks. If it had been today, I would have certainly needed stiches. I don't even remember telling my teacher about it. I guess I must have washed off the injury, but I also don't remember that. What I do remember is when I got on my bike after school, I couldn't ride it home because when I bent my knee, blood began to flow from the open wound. I pushed the bicycle the two miles home.

About ten years ago I was showing the spot to my two grandsons. Lucas stepped carefully down the rocky surface and looked back up at me. He said, "Grandpa, I see some stains on the rocks here. I bet they came from you." I didn't have the heart to tell him that after 60 plus years they had probably washed away. They certainly haven't been washed away from my memory.

Another bicycle mishap I recall was when I turned right toward the front of Eno Church. Walking toward me was Yance Riley. Mr. Yance continued toward me and I just knew he would move out of the way. He didn't and I drove my bike up his pants leg. He shouted at me with some very strong language, you probably would have, too. After grandson Lucas heard of my experience, he asked just what Mr. Riley had said. I replied,"Hot dang, you all. I swear." That wasn't exactly how it was, but it was good enough for Lucas. Have we ever really thought how those early bicycles made our world become a larger and more interesting place?

I continued to enjoy riding bicycles after I grew up and had my own children. My daughter Laura and I made frequent treks near our home in Alamance County. We sometimes took back roads all the way to Hillsborough.

A STREAK OF BLUE

A streak of blue with wistful blonde hair
Blowing in the breeze
Became a young girl perched upon her bicycle
Pedaling with such grace and ease.

"To ride in a car would be much easier,"
She thought as she traveled on morn,
"But never would I see the tiny shrew
Or hear the wind blow through the corn."

Even though her legs grew tired,
She still traveled on,
Stopping at Mann's grocery,
And then turned back toward home.

A small calf watched her
As she went by,
Grazing in the meadow
Under a beautiful blue sky.

Passing motorists returned her wave
Bathed in the sunset glow
Adding a touch of happiness
To the traffic flow.

Her mother joyfully smiled
Her dog happily barked
The kitty mewed and mewed
As the blue bike was parked.

ALL CATS GO TO HEAVEN IN THE END

It was June 4, 2006. The day before, I had buried Jasper, our cat of 14 years. He was one of those animals that became part of our family. I have a few memories that stand out.

I worked part-time at Alamance Community College as evening supervisor. One night when I arrived at work, after getting out of the van, I happened to glance back to see a cat glued to the back window. At first I thought it was one of those stuffed toys that people like to surprise people with. I was surprised to realize that it was Jasper. Evidently, he had fallen asleep in the car. I had to work about four hours. When it was time to leave I had someone distract him on side of the vehicle while I slipped into the driver's seat.

Another time my friend Dean Hall and I played a round of golf at Southwick Golf Course. When Dean got out of his car, I noticed he lowered his window a little since it was a very warm day so I did the same. When we finished a few hours later, I told Dean to be careful because there was a figure of a cat under his car. Suddenly a black cat ran out and under another parked vehicle. I knew it couldn't be Jasper but I called, "Kitty, kitty," anyway. Guess what, he came running. I guess he had again fallen asleep in the back seat and then crawled out the open window when he awoke. How close I had come to losing him right there. If I had not spotted him under the parked car I would have driven away and perhaps never seen him again.

My grandsons, Nicholas and Lucas, joined us around the grave as we said our last good-byes. Nicholas said that Jasper was now in cat heaven. He had just turned six. Three-year-old Lucas began to wonder out loud. "Grandpa, is there a bumble bee heaven?" We had just seen one that had bitten the dust earlier that day. Lucas was then on a roll. "How about a bird heaven or a bug heaven? Do you think there could be a camel cricket heaven?"

Nicholas, standing near his mom said, "Mama, when Grandpa dies, I bet he will have a lot of yellow labs like Dezzie (our beloved lab) to be with him." You know, I would settle for that. What could be better?

Nicholas, me, and Dezzie on one of many adventures.

Jasper the cat.

A LESSON FROM LUCAS

Lynda and I used to take the grandsons to the library every Saturday. When Lucas was about three and a half and Nicholas about seven, we were headed to the library on Memorial Day weekend. I wasn't sure the library would be open. I felt more

 apprehensive when two good parking places were available. Lynda and Nicholas got out of the car and walked to the door. It opened so I got out and walked about 100 feet to the entrance. Lynda looked back and yelled, "Lucas!" I realized that I had left him in the car. Rushing back with my heart in my throat, I opened the door to find him getting teary.

"Why did you leave me?"
I guess that question will always be with me. Walking into the library, Lucas was holding my hand. I was still shaken over what had just transpired. He looked up at me and said,

"Grandpa, you are not very smart."
He was right and I put that one down in the "never forget" room of my memories.

Lucas and I at Grandparents' Day at Front Street Playschool, Burlington, NC

TREES ARE MADE FOR PEOPLE LIKE ME

Joyce Kilmer wrote, "I think I shall never see a poem as lovely as a tree." For years I thought the most interesting part about that was that Joyce Kilmer was a guy. As time passed, however, I began to realize just how important trees have been. We had a cherry tree in our front yard in West Hillsborough and I would climb to the top of it. On a day with a stiff breeze one would get a really good ride. From the top of that tree, I could see a good deal of my neighborhood.

Looking down the hill to the east I could see Alec Riley's store building. I always thought it was interesting that the little branch ran directly under it. Did it ever rain enough to flood the store? Oh, that store is where I used to get those delicious candy orange slices.

The tree also gave me a view of Jones Avenue that went up the hill from Eno Street to our elementary school. Mr. Ben Terrell used to have a little store on the left side about halfway up the hill. It was within walking distance to school. Actually, everything was within walking distance. There used to be a teacher who sometimes after lunch, would send a student down to Mr. Terrell's store to get a package of BC powder. I guess teaching then was as stressful as it is today. She had to take a BC to help her get through the rest of the day.

Another favorite tree of mine was the apple tree out behind Eno United Methodist Church. I remember climbing it and dropping "bombs" on the enemy below. I'm sure that was at the end of World War II.

I was thinking that children don't climb trees as much today, but I can picture daughter Laura and her cousin Jason Coleman perched in a little dogwood in Bryant "Pa" Brewer's yard in Fairview. Lynda remembers our two grandsons scampering up a tree at the Woods' family beach house. Joyce Kilmer said in "Trees" that "poems are made by fools like me and that "only God can make a tree." I just hope he makes some more accessible for the kids of today.

Nicholas in a tree at Mike Woods' place.

HEARING IS NOT THE SAME AS LISTENING

Several years ago my nephew Paul Coleman asked an interesting question. He was about 10 years old and we were moving Edith Brewer, better known to the grandkids as Nana, from her house in Fairview to her apartment next to her sister Eloise Thompson, better known as Sally.

Paul was in the back seat as I was backing out with another load of odds and ends when he said, "Charles, did Jesus smoke a pipe?"

"Paul, I responded, that is a very profound question."
That minute long conversation became an integral part of family get-togethers each year around Christmas. Paul and the other cousins just wouldn't let it go. You see, Paul said that the question he asked was actually, "Charles, did you ever smoke a pipe?" Okay he was in the back seat and I have a definite hearing problem.

I have carried it with me for as long as I remember. I don't think I was dropped on my head as a small child, but I did have pneumonia and chicken pox accompanied with some high fevers. Years later as an adult and taking a hearing test, I discovered just how bad it was. So that is why coaches were so concerned that I ran wrong patterns on the football field. Could you imagine wearing a football helmet and someone calling plays but something was missing from the communication?

Doctors told me that my problem was nerve damage and a hearing aid would just distort the sounds coming my way. Later, my youngest daughter, Laura was studying to be a speech pathologist. She said, "Dad things have changed over the years. I think you should see an audiologist."

I set up an appointment and wow was I surprised. The result was a hearing aid that opened a brand new world for me. The first thing I was aware of was the sound of the gravel beneath my feet in the driveway, and the birds – I hear them now. I will forever be indebted to Laura Stanley Khorozov. Lynda said that I may not have a hearing problem now but that I still have a listening problem, especially when it comes to taking out the trash.

THE GIFT OF SONG GLADDENS OUR HEARTS

Most people have never heard me sing. I really only do it while mowing or in the shower. I do sing at church but only during congregational songs. I've never sung in the choir but I have been asked from time to time to narrate a cantata. I sometimes think that's because someone is afraid that I may volunteer to sing in it. I do, however, have a great appreciation of music and musicians. The following are names that hold or bring back musical memories.

Alma Andrews. Someone said the gift of song is the gift of love. Alma sang mostly at Eno United Methodist Church. Her solos were the first I ever experienced. She sang at weddings (ours included), Homecoming, Sunday services, and funerals. There was no "American Idol, "America's Got Talent, or "The Voice" then but if she could have entered, judges would have been blown away.

Hazel Thompson Parker. I don't ever remember hearing Alma sing when she wasn't accompanied by Hazel on the piano. Her unique touch of piano keys was only equaled by the gentle softness of her voice.

Hazel Parker accompanying Alma Andrews at Eno United Methodist Church

Lewis Thompson. Now if you want to hear a piano performance, you have to hear Lewis. He is my wife's uncle. A joy of past holiday seasons was to hear him at our family Christmas Eve Eve (that's the day before Christmas Eve) get-togethers. I got a great email from Bob Scarlett, a West Hillsboro native, who performed with Lewis in the Ambassador Quartet in the early 50's. They had a live radio program each Sunday at a station in Durham. Bob remarked that Lewis was the only piano player he knew who could play by reading the notes or play by ear. Lewis was known from West Hillsborough throughout North Carolina.

Lewis on the keyboard at a Christmas Eve party at Robin Brewer's home.

Lewis with sisters Edith and Eloise in front of Eno United Methodist Church

Paul Wilson. Paul was from Alamance County and attended Bellemont United Methodist Church where Lynda and I go to church since moving to Burlington. Paul could play about any type of string instrument but he could make a mandolin talk. You could feel the music through his instrument and the smile on his face.

I have to proudly mention the performers in our immediate family. My daughter Carol Stanley who sang in special choral groups and musicals while in high school recently received a UNC Greensboro Outstanding Alumni recognition based on her service as President of the Georgia Library Association. Carol does not usually sing in her duties as President but she does put on amazing character performances during the annual scholarship program. She has been Susan Boyle from "America's Got Talent" fame and Effie Trinket from the "Hunger Games" books and movies. Carol is quite an entertainer.

Younger daughter, Laura sang from the time she was six years old. She was "Annie" in a school musical and Alamance County's Junior Miss in 12th grade. Laura later sang on a cruise ship out of Fort Lauderdale where she sang her way into the heart of her future husband, Edward Khorozov, who worked on the ship as well.

Standing in the wings is the next generation of musicians that make up my world of appreciation: my grandson Nicholas Khorozov is quite a drummer. His brother, Lucas received a number of high ratings from his piano recitals. I think the humanity within each of us is open to the sounds of harmony. My vocal cords are limited but my heart sings!

Laura crowned Miss Southern High School, 1989

Lucas in a piano recital held by his piano teacher, Mrs. Sarah House, at Elon University

**Nicholas playing the drums for his grandmother,
Tatyana Khorozova, visiting from Ukraine.**

RECONNECTING WITH OLD FRIENDS IMPORTANT

A few years back I included some of these ponderings and reminiscing in the News of Orange County. It was a great experience because I reconnected with a lot of old friends. Here is one from October, 2012

John Horne and I were good friends in high school. While thinking about some of our adventures – mostly involving his old Chevrolet-it dawned on me there were several holes in my memory. It was more than 50 years ago. Maybe I earned those lapses.

So I remember being out on Old N.C. 86 somewhere between Hillsborough and Chapel Hill. John's car had broken down and I can still see moonlight reflecting off the winding road as a whole carload of us teenagers were meandering toward nowhere. So what happened after that? John now lives in Burlington. We actually haven't seen each other in 50 plus year, so I gave him a call today and asked how we got out of that particular predicament. We had a great reunion over the phone. John thinks we made our way to Glenn and Don Collins' house and they helped us get back home. The Collins family owned a dairy farm out on 86. I remembered another time when his headlights went out and really messed up an evening of planned merriment.

The most trouble we got into was not because the car malfunctioned, but one day when it performed perfectly. My senior year at Hillsboro High School included two study halls after lunch. One day, John suggested that we go home. Since I had no afternoon classes, his suggestion seemed very reasonable. He was parked right in front of the school. We got in and pulled out of the spot. As we drove away, I thought, "What a great idea!"

Now, Mr. Childress, the school janitor did his job by going to Mr. Grady Brown, our principal and immediately reporting the skipping incident. The resulting penalty was that we could not return to school unless accompanied by a parent. One could imagine how embarrassed my mom was. John relayed to me on the phone that his punishment continued when his father addressed his backside when he finally got home. I don't remember a similar disciplinary action, but I think some of my family thought it was kind of funny. Not me.

Looking back in the 1957 football season, John Horne completed two passes out of seven attempts. The interesting stat is that both completions were for touchdowns. John, you did well. Some of you had great friends while in high school, and have never seen or contacted them since. Do a good deed for them and yourself. Give them a call. Also plan on going to your next reunion.

Another article from October 2012 had a similar theme of holes in memories and reconnecting with people from our past.

COLAND RILEY A STAPLE IN THE COMMUNITY

Do you remember where you first pumped gas into your car? How about the first time you heard of a bomb shelter? Many questions of my past are full of blanks when trying to fill in the empty spaces. Some come back rather vividly.

My family mostly frequented Coland's and Betty Riley's stores. What I remember about him was that the store is the only place I ever saw him and his wife, Blanche. In my early years and even later, he was always there.

I guess we all look for constants in our lives, especially today. Just think, that was years before the supermarkets and big box stores. I wanted more information regarding Coland. Did he have the first gas pump in West Hillsborough? Did he really have a bomb shelter under his house? I called my friend Butch Raynor who later ran a convenience store just north on West Hill Avenue and posed those questions to him. Now, Butch is a legend in his own time and has bountiful knowledge of his neighborhood. I asked whatever happened to Doris, Coland's daughter? Butch replied, "She lives up there in Alamance County near you somewhere." In about five minutes of research (the internet is awesome), I located Doris who actually lives about a half a mile away.

We had a great conversation. She thinks the first gas pump in West Hillsborough was at her grandfather Alec Riley's store. I could see the store building from the top of my front yard cherry tree. She also concurred that the little stream did run directly under the store.

She remembers that she and her cousin, Danny Ray Melton looked for crawfish under rocks there. Just think, about 200 yards west I was doing the same thing under the big poplar tree across the road from Jim Faucette's house. I wonder if she ever saw my bark boats floating by. I wonder if children today look for crawfish in nearby streams. Just turning over a rock and waiting for the water to clear was an adventure in itself. There he would be, with those pincers ready to take on the giant foe who had invaded his domain. You had to be careful and pick him up behind those pincers or you could get a painful pinch.

Coland Riley was probably the first businessman I ever knew. When Cone Mill sold the houses of the mill village, he bought several and used them for rental property. And yes—according to Butch, Doris, Reggie Vick, and others- he did have a bomb shelter filled with food and water. He was a survivalist during the Cold War that thank goodness never became hot.

It seems that every time I turn around I run into a former Hillsborough or Orange County friend here in Alamance County. Actually, Alamance County was formed out of Orange County in 1849 according to Dr. Powell's Encyclopedia of North Carolina. I guess we kind of just spilled over into what was ours up until that date. Reggie Vick, Ann Craven, Brent Wilder and Doris Riley are just a few transplants. To me the most amazing fact is that while waiting in line to pick up grandson Nicholas at Southern Alamance Middle School, two cars behind me one can find a couple who entered West Hillsboro Elementary School the same time I did – James and June Taylor awaiting their middle school grandson.

Wait there's more, Barbara Davis, Grady Brown's niece lived within a half mile and attended the same church as Lynda and I do. Judy Ward Parker is found there also on Sundays. John Horne and I communicate occasionally. Clem Johnson lives in Graham. Peggy Minnis Brown, Harry Neal Brown and Lynda's sister Harriett Brewer also relocated here. I'm sure there are more and if any of you didn't want to be found, I express my sincere apologies.

The former store of Coland Riley on West Hill Avenue, Hillsboro, NC

REMEMBERING THE SOUNDS OF HILLSBOROUGH WEST

There are many sounds that take us back years to the places of our younger times. Waking up in the morning or going to sleep at night to the gentle rain on our tin roof is certainly one. The pounding earth-shaking vibrations of passing trains will always be a part of us. Living about a half mile from the Eno Cotton Mill brought the abrupt sound from the weave room when someone opened an outside door. Equally shattering was the sudden silence when that door was closed. Church bells on Sunday morning brought sounds all so familiar as to the direction of our life journeys. Some of us never thought we had a choice but to go; the same as the school bells, each reminding us that there was something above and beyond us. The sound of bare feet crossing the river bridge near the mill, and the voice of the Eno as it passed over the dam below are part of our tapestry. Somebody's rooster crowing, a whip-o-will giving its lonely cry, and a bobwhite's pleasant call – when was the last time you heard any of those? They are all etched in our minds.

How familiar were the sounds of play? A bat connecting with a ball, a ball bouncing off the roof of the church or against the brick foundation, the "umph" sound of someone being tackled on the church lawn on a cool autumn afternoon, and the sound of tennis shoes hitting the cold pavement while a group of teenagers were playing football awaiting the school bus at Brooks' store on a frigid January morning.

Probably the best sound was Mom calling for us to come in to supper. That happened every evening from the Mountain village, to the Old and New Hill, and down to Monkey Bottom.

The sounds, smells, people and experiences that shaped me have inspired a lot of pondering over these 77 years. I often have taken to the page to attempt to put into words, feelings that were inspired by my beginnings in West Hillsborough, College, Family and beyond.

POEMS AND REMEMBRANCES

"PEOPLE, PLACES, AND IDEAS INSPIRED BY A LIFE FIRST ROOTED ON THE OCCONEECHEE MOUNTAIN OF HILLSBOROUGH, NC"

THE IMAGE OF GOD

God's first image in my mind
Came many years ago;
In Sunday School I sat resigned
Awaiting that which I should know.

He appeared with long flowing hair
And a splendid robe of white,
Gliding wondrously through the air
Watching over us both day and night.

And years passed

I remember a revival here
When on one hot summer night
I pictured God not just with fear
But something close to extreme fright.

Phillips I believe was his name
And he preached brimstone and smoke
So another image of God then came
When Revelation and Phillips spoke.

And years passed

Teen age is fleeting youth;
A time to search, a time to ask...
Who is God? What is truth?
The MYF appeared to aid the task.

Worship, a campfire; and evening breeze;
Games, friends: old and new
I found God in all of those.
Another image came into view.

And years passed

In college God became so vast.
Omnipotent, universal--Tillich, Neibur, and Kant
Could I rely on images of the Past?
Was he alive? Dead? or how relevant.

I saw God as challenge; God as Quest;
God as both question and reply;
God as growth; God as rest.
But most of all as Love--what more for you or I.

And years passed

Often now I'll open the door
That takes me back to when I was four;
And again He appears with long flowing hair
And a splendid robe of white
Gliding wondrously through the air
Watching over us both day and night.

Sometimes, one feels irritated by the religious double standard: Self comfort or sacrificing service. Being aware of this paradox, words just seemed to flow:

COMFORT SIN

Father, we come to this nice place
Withe central heat and cool air, too.
All unpleasantness please erase
So we may worship You.

The music is really great
The flowers smell so sweet.
It's so easy to meditate
Especially from my cushioned seat.

The stained glass lets in radiant hue.
What a truly inspiring sight.
It's so nice to be here with You
Where everything is holy and right.

Somewhere outside, knocking I hear.
I wish he would go away.
Good Heavens, this noise I fear
Will cause my concentration to stray.

And so you knock outside the hall
And ask to be let in
Will we ever heed your call
And be saved from Comfort Sin?

SALLY REMEMBERED

Sally Thompson Melton Oakley was the sister of Edith Thompson Brewer. Sally was married first to Ervin Melton and years after his death, married Wayne Oakley. She played an interesting role in the community. At wakes someone always spent the night in the home of the deceased or welcomed visitors. Sally was there for West Hillsborough families. She was someone to depend upon. I remember her for that and the simple faith and dedication to her family, church, and community.

SALLY SAID GRACE

There is a moment between the food arriving on my plate
And from there to my face
That I suddenly hesitate
And hear the simple words, "Who is going to say Grace?"

Whether it was KFC or the Colonial Inn
Or a large gathering spilling over into the den;
Whether it was my house or your place
The question remained, "Who is going to say Grace?"

Sally really said "ask the blessing,"
But I couldn't make that rhyme
But whether it was a "mater" sandwich or chicken dressing
She reminded us every single time.

After every meal she ate in town
Sally got up and visited all around.
At almost every table there was someone she knew
And she wouldn't leave until she was through.

I have had a few meals since she passed,
And I hesitate before going to my plate.
My prayer is one of thanks
For being Graced and Blessed by our Sally.

Sally stood by many in their grief
And shared laughter on brighter days.
She was an example of the wonderful belief
That signifies the meaning of True Church ways.

Edith Brewer was my mother-in-law and a pillar to her family and all of those who knew her.

NANA

On a snowy winter day
I met her daughter half way
Between West Hill and Fairview
The footprints then went two by two
To the warmth of the Brewer home.

She greeted and welcomed me in.
My future "Pa" was in the den.
She got me out of my shoes so wet
And then did a deed I will never forget
In the warmth of the Brewer home.

She brought out slippers of her own,
And years later after I was grown
And was one of the sons her daughters would choose
I am honored to have walked in my Nana's shoes
In the warmth of the Brewer home.

WHAT MATTERS

When I used to hitch a ride
And venture forward with a thrill
I wondered when I finally died
Would it be another adventure still?

Last week in our lesson we read
That when we're dead, we're really dead.
What happened to my often thought plan
That my spirit escaped and looked down on my clan?

Gee, I thought Jesus raised Lazarus, his friend.
Now I'm told there was a different end.
That he really resuscitated him from his grave,
Do I need to re-program my thoughts once again?

Let not your hearts be troubled any more.
I have prepared you a dwelling place you see;
And when you get to the Father's distant shore
When you cross life's portal by going through me

Now comes the "many mansions" part
Chuck and I and perhaps some more
Have for years held in our heart
Thoughts there were rooms with our names on the door.

He has prepared us a place
Jesus left us through the cross
To give us a life to misfortune face
And to know God and his wonderful Grace.

Thomas asked "Lord, where are you to go?
Because we surely don't know the way."
Two thousand years later, we aren't sure and we want to know
Are we missing His point, even today?

Jesus said, "I am the way."
Phillip said, "Show us the Father."
Then Phillip, you, and I will be ok
Then Jesus said to us, "When you see me you also see my Father."

Perhaps our mission is becoming clear
So now we know why we are sitting here
"Into my heart; Come into my heart Lord Jesus
Come in today; come in to stay

And let my little light shine
Let it shine, Let it shine
So who then may see our light
May also see the father more clearly.

February 2007

EDUCATION

I came out of the night
Searching, longing for a goal.
Please teach me right
Lest I return to the hole.

I came from nowhere
And the path led here.
Please show me somewhere
Or I shall always fear.

Please give me a light
With which I will go
Thought filled with fright
Back into the hole.

As I travel beyond your wall,
With my light I now see
That it wasn't a hole at all
But a gentle valley.

THE TEACHER

Today I ventured into a new world
One untamed, restless and wild.
Wonder upon wonders were to me unfurled
For today I taught a child.

Many vain attempts I had made
And I struggled all the while
Now I am both relieved and afraid
For today I taught a child

MOTIVATION

The world awaits
Youth's unborn skills
The vast potential traits
That lie dormant still

Somewhere there is a key
That fits a certain door
Setting a young mind free
Giving enlightenment forever more

Free to travel the road of life
The ever challenging walkway
It doesn't eliminate strife
Only brightens the pathway.

I FEEL AMERICA GROWING

I feel America growing.
The workers are in the field.
Seeds for tomorrow they are sowing.
There should be a plentiful yield.

God gave us a period to live
And a time-space to cherish.
We must plan; we must build,
For without vision we perish.

Friends as we fellowship beneath the tree;
As we eat, and laugh, and play,
Let us not take for granted that we are free.
It's not by chance that we celebrate today.

I feel America growing—
The torch of Freedom has been passed.
Remember, we are the heirs.
Time is moving so very fast.
Soon we'll hand it to our children; the task will be theirs.

LAURA AT FOUR

She pranced merrily into the bakery door,
With dancing eyes and voice of glee.
"On October first I will be four.
Will you please fix a pink cake for me?"

"To decorate I'll need your name,"
"Of course, Ma'am; It's Laura Michelle,
I'm so glad my birthday came.
Just put Laura – the rest is hard to spell."

A frown creased her tiny brow
As we walked from the store.
"Can't we take now?"
"No it's for the party Saturday at four."

Kim, Jason, Mandy, and Teresa, too
Smiles, candles, and cake;
Presents, games-dreams come true
And all the pictures Mom will make

LAURA AT FIVE

The morning sun gleams in her hair
While waiting for the bus.
Her smile, her skin so fair-
Does she really belong to us?

Greeting everyone with, "Hi, I'm five.
Watch me ride my bike!"
So vibrant, fluid, Oh-ALIVE!
There is a world to be found by that tyke.

BICYCLES

Bicycles on a sweet spring day
Interweaving through valley and field
Carry daughter and me on our way.
Young and old have ties to build.
Clear is the blue sky above,
Lending happy moments for future rhyme.
Events that create boundless love
Should remain through endless time.

THE PHOTOGRAPH

The click of the shutter and flash of light
Holds time suspended for us to behold;
And keeps it from passing in mind's flight
Allowing clouded memories to visually unfold.

SLEEP

Sleep is the thief of life,
It steals our days and encroaches on tomorrows.
It smothers precious thoughts at night
And hides surprises from eager eyes.

Sleep, I hate you true,
You enemy of the brilliant dawn.
Daylight will soon overpower you
As it spreads upon my lawn.

I lose to you each night
And break your bonds at dawn,
And later when I think I have won
I am humbled with a yawn.

CHALLENGE

Change the world or a part of it;
Attack the body or the heart of it.
Do not quibble over what to do.
Just get on with it
    And
        Work
            Until
                You
                    Are
                        Through!

VISION

Life today was joy and sorrow
The same lies in every tomorrow

AMERICAN VIGIL

The stripe of gold around the tree
Faded as the seasons passed.
Hope in the hearts of those who waited
Pulsed in common – a nation of heartbeats.

200 million gathered at the sturdy oak.
In silent vigil no one spoke.
It was our hurt, our burden to bear.
We chose to be there, we chose to care.

We came with candles, hope and prayer.
We became stronger-Americans had goals to share.
52 were hostages in an alien land,
Tightly held captive by revolution's hand.

Then came the freedom day
We all heard our herald say
"And that's the way it is January 20th, 1981."
A day of release for everyone.

PARENTS

Parents come in all shapes and sizes
That is obvious and plain to see
As one ponders and surmises
He or she may discover a few surprises
Mainly from you or from me.

Parents once were into any new rages
I know you find it hard to realize
That these wise advice giving sages
Were seeing the same concerns in their mom's eyes.

Why do parents sometimes try to rule?
Perhaps they are afraid you will roam.
You can't learn this present job at school
Many learned from living in their home.

There is a fine line that parents walk
When do I protect? When do I let go?
It is so important that you sit and talk.
There is so much to understand and know.

The responsibility is so immense.
The shaping of the world to come.
Emotions erupting are so very intense.
How important this role has become.

Be thankful for friends and good fellowship.
Small group discussions and self-realization
In a country where we are free to worship
And prepare parents for the next generation.

THE WEB OF LIFE

Behold the web of early fall
Glistening about its ageing master
Within there is meaning for all
As time moves on faster—faster.

It spans a vast chasm from tree to tree
And gently shimmers in the wind,
Becoming a basket for leaves set free
And a task for the maker to mend

The creator moves more slowly now
The weight of age can be seen.
She retreats to the sheltered bow
And views the tattered screen.

As men we see as dust
Creation by web, hand, or mind.
It is thereby right and just;
All life is thus entwined.

There is a slender thread
Running through us all.
Time is a road each will tread
From spring to summer to fall.

In moments of loss I take to the page to reflect on things that will never make sense. When daughter Carol's dear friend passed I wrote this reflection. I think of the Freeland family and honor them.

LORI

Lori, we hardly knew you.
So swift life does part
As the drops of morning dew
You linger within the heart.

Oh lover of life
Whose taste was so brief,
Peace in a world of strife
We share in familial grief.

Footprints in sands of time;
The journey was at the start.
Erased – was there reason or rhyme?
They linger within the heart.

The cries of those who care;
The "whys" from those who love.
The loss is more to bear.
Where is the peace from above?

When my friend Joe Dickey lost his wife I again took to the page.

JEANETTE

Little girls, please don't weep;
Your mother has but gone to sleep.
She was here briefly, it's true;
But she blessed the world with you.

Young man growing strong and true.
She will certainly be missed by you.
With you here there will be no good-byes
For she left herself in your eyes.

And to you who shared her life
Together as husband and wife
Words cannot express how we feel.
To us all, she was sincere – she was real.

THE BOX

THE BOX KEEPS MY

WORDS FROM

FLOWING FREELY

UNINHIBITED OUT

INTO THE

WONDERFUL

UNKNOWN. PLEASE

REMOVE THE

BOUNDARIES TO MY

CREATIVE

EXPRESSION

A VALENTINE REFLECTION

Valentine's Day is occasion for rhyme.
Verse should have a special time;
But at 7:00AM on the day
Longfellow wouldn't know what to say.

When you come to the end of the day
And beside each other lay
Love, your home is adorning
If you love to look at him or her in the morning.

Before he shaved and combed with care;
Before she took the curlers from her hair,
Did you say, "I love you without end.
Let's go eat breakfast with the Methodist Men."

THE UKRAINA

The ship that brought Edward and Laura together
To sail in balmy and stormy weather
Plays a role as we gather under these trees today;
Even in the absence of rolling sea and foamy spray

Great ship, you took Edward to many parts and places;
Africa, South America, Europe and Asia faces,
But he never knew the supreme destiny when you set sail
For the beautiful exotic sea and sand of Fort Lauderdale

To the proud vessel I raise my glass
For bringing together this lad and lass;
For keeping Edward safe for his unknown fate,
And making Laura's "Sea Escape" into a wedding date.

**SeaEscape aka "The Ukraina" docked
in Fort Lauderdale, Florida**

NOVEMBER ANNOUNCEMENT

Hello, We haven't met
Because you haven't come to us;
At least not yet;
But already you are causing quite a fuss.

Your mother said she saw you today
When she and dad were at the doctor place;
Some kind of sonar ray
You danced and jumped and made a face.

Grandma Lynda and Grandpa Charles can't sleep.
They stay awake thinking about you each night,
And are counting baby names instead of sheep;
And pray in their prayers that the Lord holds you tight.

A LETTER TO NICHOLAS

September 12, 2001

Dear Nicholas,

Yesterday, 9/11/01, a great tragedy happened in the United States of America. We have been told that our world will never be the same again. Several terrorists took over four airplanes and crashed them into important buildings in our country. Two crashed into the twin towers of the World Trade Center in New York City. Another crashed into the Pentagon, the headquarters of our country's military. Another never made it to any important buildings. Several very brave men overcame and the terrorists and the plane crashed killing all occupants but saving perhaps countless others. Thousands were killed in the two buildings and hundreds at the Pentagon. As I write this, the final tally of those dead has not been completed. The two buildings both over 100 stories high, collapsed soon after the impacts. This occurred about 8:30 in the morning and all people were not at work. On a given day 50,000 people worked in the buildings. There are several heroic stories of people saving lives. Many emergency workers, firemen and police when killed when the towers collapsed. It has been a very troubling time for all of us. This morning I placed the American flag on my porch in memory of those who died and as a symbol that our country was shaken but not shattered.

Your mom called me yesterday from Dania Beach, your first home, and we talked about the horror of it all. You were with your babysitter Mrs. Grace. I am sorry that my first letter to you was about this, but it might someday be important to you. The news people are saying that our world will never be the same. My hope for you is that your world will be brighter and better than ours is at this moment in time. Tonight I wish I had a crystal ball to look into and be encouraged by the future in which you live.

Your Grandma Lynda and I love you and your parents very much. Sleep well.

Your Grandpa Charles

THERE'S A LIZARD IN THE LIBRARY

Mrs. Stanley works in the library.
She came to school early one day.
Now libraries are not often scary,
But a surprise sometimes comes our way.

It was early and the Snow Camp dew
Covered the grass as she parked in her space.
Did you ever wonder if someone was watching you,
But never showed his or her face? – This was such a day.

Our librarian unlocked her door
And it opened with a rusted "SQUEEK."
Did something scurry across the floor?
Perhaps she would take a little peek.

No there was nothing there at all
She wondered just what it could be,
"Oh, it was just a draft from the hall
And I was just imagining, silly me."

A book mark lay curvy on a shelf.
"Who would leave one there?" she mused.
"I told them over and over and then repeated myself,
A bookmark should be used."

She reached and suddenly the curvy mark was gone.
"This is very mysterious." She said to no one at all.
And then she was no longer all alone;
The kindergarten marched quietly in from the hall.

A fly flew through the door as the class made its way.
Mrs. Stanley saw it on her pretty decorated wall.
She jumped up to get her swatter intending to mash his day,
But returned to see that it was gone. Had he been there at all?

Johnny was looking high and low for a book to take home.
"Mrs. Stanley, Mrs. Stanley, I see what I want to take!"
His librarian was relieved for all the aisles he would roam.
"I want to know all about creepy, crawly things like a snake,
But most of all I want to read about a lizard
LIKE THE ONE THAT LIVES IN MY LIBRARY!"

PEACE

Tonight I felt you very near.
We spoke of life and fear;
And quietly of death and tear,
Then we both laughed and felt secure.

LAST LETTER FROM APPALACHIAN

It is tattered and it is torn,
The edges are blemished and worn.
Some people carry valuable things in a locket;
I have carried your letter 43 years in my pocket.

"Hello Darling," was the opening salutation.
You then remarked about my upcoming graduation,
And then about the most important thing you said,
"The very best part is that we will soon be wed."

I especially like the "I love you." You said it twice.
And the "Forever Yours" was especially nice.
Looking back over all the laughter and tears
Those words have held us for so many years.

We have celebrated our silver and will hopefully our gold,
But for our 43rd if it is ok to be so bold
To just say simply our love couldn't be better
Than that expressed in your last Appalachian letter.

HAPPY ANNIVERSARY, DARLING

Charles
8/18/2005

We had a wonderful All Hillsboro High School Reunion, April 30, 2011 and again on May 18, 2013. I wrote this poem in remembrance of our school.

YOU CAME BACK TO ME

I nurtured you.
I gave you fledgling wings to fly.
I believed in you when others scoffed.
Your mind traveled while reading my books.
"There is no galleon like a book to take you lands away."
I made your world a bigger and better place.

And you came back to me.

You were mine for a short while,
But you took a part of me with you.
Your stories were often my stories.
Some found your soul mates in my shadow.
You call yourself Class of '48 or maybe '58.
I remember you as a class of "One!"
One school; one high school; one Hillsboro High.

And you came back to me.

Hillsboro High School, 1958

OLD MAN HOLT

The mist roamed the night
Searching for a place to dwell.
It finally found a place to light
And dropped drearily into the dell.

Now completely free
The moon shone upon the glade,
Bouncing beams from tree to tree;
To every branch and blade.

A figure broke the hill's crest,
A small bent frame,
Often coming to needed rest
With labor leaning on a cane.

Old Man Holt stood alone
On the quiet moonlit lea
And uttered a tired groan;
He was eighty-three.

There in the depths of night
Was a man coming home.
For this was the ancient site
Of the old king's throne.

The hearth was now only ash
Prodded by his cane pole,
To others it was cold trash;
To him it burned alive in his soul

Here a fire warmed his young
And welcomed all men,
Here many songs were sung.
Those days seemed only yesterday – then

Far below were city lights
Where whippoorwills once nested
From these lofty heights
Holt watched while he rested.

A moonlit tear glistened brightly on his cheek
As he leaned upon his cane.
This was his first visit in a week;
Old Holt would not come again.

The crippled figure passed from view
Leaving behind the moon above,
And the still, quiet blades of dew
While taking with him so many years of love.

THE CABOOSE

As we approach the end of this collection of thoughts and stories I am reminded of the disappearing caboose.

One of the simple joys of my childhood was to listen for the train, and when I heard its distant rumble, I would tear out my back door and head for the Eno United Methodist Church yard. There, while standing fewer than 100 yards from the train, I would wave at the engineer and start counting. The most cars I ever counted was probably about 180. That was a lot of America moving.

At the rear of the train was the caboose. I waved and the railroad men riding in it waved back. I then hurried home, leaping over the hedge bordering the church parsonage. You know, I miss that caboose. One of the first songs I sang in elementary school went like this, "Little red caboose, chug, chug, chug. Going down the track, track, track. Little red caboose behind the train."

I guess children don't sing that anymore because it isn't there. There is something wrong when trains have no end to them. The caboose always gave a punctuation mark to the train's journey when it passed before my eyes. Now it always looks like something is missing. In fact if you observe closely, there are hoses and all kinds of coupling hanging out behind the final car.

Oh you can find cabooses now if you look for them. Usually they are located in city parks or sometimes, like in Burlington, you can find one downtown across the tracks from the new depot. Children love to clamber up on them and there seems to be some kind of magnetism between the two. Maybe it is the thrill of being on a real train. Probably most kids have never ridden on a train or seen a little red caboose behind one.

Hang in there caboose. There are some of us that hope to see you giving finality to every passing freight. Trains, like most of the stories we like, should have happy endings. After riding a freight through Glacier National Park and falling off of it in Minot, North Dakota, I somehow had a happy ending; and the last thing I saw was the little red caboose going out of sight.

All good things come to an end

West Hillsborough Origins

CHARLES B. STANLEY

In "Alice's Adventures in Wonderland," the white rabbit put on his spectacles.

"Where shall I begin, please, your Majesty?" he asked.

"Begin at the beginning," the king said gravely. "And go on till you come to the end.

"Then stop."

For the past year, we have visited the Eno River and its impact on our lives. We've climbed the Occoneechee Mountain and even peered into the Panther's Den.

We have sat on the steps of Eno United Methodist Church and watched the train go by.

We were nurtured by the personalities of our past grounded in the Cone Mill cotton mill village of West Hillsboro. There was a story in each of the 150 mill houses, and we carry those memories with us.

This is my last column—maybe I shouldn't ever say never.

I want to thank the News of Orange and its staff, especially Keith Coleman and Vanessa Shortley, for giving me the opportunity to share a moment in time for a good number of friends and acquaintances.

Here's hoping for a happy holiday season and a healthy New Year.

Charles B. Stanley is a former resident of West Hillsborough. He can be reached at charles_stanley@bellsouth.net.

My last article in the News of Orange

The caboose in downtown Burlington, North Carolina

ACKNOWLEDGEMENTS

Someone said there is a story in every car one meets on the highway of life. Wait a minute – I said that.

When I came into my family of half-sisters and brother, they were at least 10 years older than me. Frances, the oldest had a love of reading and passed that on to me. Phyliss was in the background supporting and encouraging. Thomas introduced me to the world of sports that years later would include a major in Physical Education and Social Studies. Mary Lou became the first woman supervisor at the Cone Mill Eno plant. She once told me, "A rolling stone gathers no moss." She was persevering and showed me I could be anything if I tried. My mother, Myrtle Ray Medlin Stanley, lived a life of sacrifice for me and the rest of her progeny. My father, Charles Bell Stanley, Sr. was highly respected in his community and was a pretty good checker player.

My immediate family is highlighted by Lynda Brewer Stanley, my wife of 55 years. She has been there at every turn in my life road, never taking any easier routes. Daughter, Carol Lynn Stanley, has forever believed I could be published. She even took a series of my poems and had them bound for my 60th birthday. Daughter Laura Stanley Khorozov's dancing fingers transferred years of my writing onto the computer and flash drive helping greatly in bringing this "epic" to fruition.

A special thanks is in order to The News of Orange County and present editor Adam Powell, past editor Keith Coleman, and Vanessa Shortly for taking my contributed articles and sharing them with the community. The response was overwhelming.

Ann Steele, a member of the Reid Brown Sunday School class at Bellemont United Methodist Church in Burlington would often exclaim to another member, "He is writing a book!" When I really wasn't. I had only shared some quote. She never let me forget that it was somewhere in my head.

Wayne Drumheller,author, publisher, professional photographer, and world traveler, showed both patience and encouragement in putting everything together and making a distant dream become a reality.

About the Author

Charles B. Stanley grew up in the small textile community of West Hillsborough between two mill villages, Belleview and the Eno Plant of Cone Mills. His early education was at West Hillsboro Elementary school and then Hillsboro High School.

Charles' post-secondary undergraduate experience was at Appalachian State Teachers' College with a degree in Physical Education and Social Studies. At Appalachian he was president of the Wesley Foundation, a Methodist student group, and later vice president of the North Carolina Methodist Student Movement. He was elected to Appalachian's Student Government Association and served on the judicial branch. Charles was also a residential assistant in his dorm.

Charles was a history and PE teacher at Southern Alamance High School where he was the first wrestling coach and coached golf before he had ever stepped on a golf course. Charles received his Masters of Education in School Counseling from UNC-Chapel Hill. He became school counselor and served in that capacity for the last twenty-five years of his professional career. He served on the executive committee of the North Carolina School Counselor Association and was recipient of the Luther Taff State School Counselor of the Year Award. Charles retired from education in 1995 and is happy to report that there is life after high school.

Charles and Lynda at Crater Lake, 2007

Notes

Notes

Notes

Notes

Notes